The

Psychological Edge

Strategies For Everyday Living

Samuel T. Shein, Ph.D.

Clinical Psychologist

Long Dash Books

Printed by:

InstaBook Maker ™

All rights reserved

InstaBooks are distributed and printed through:

Long Dash Publishing

49 Orchard Street

Hackensack NJ 07601

For more information:

www.longdash.com

Acknowledgements

Where do you begin to thank all the people in your life who have contributed to the making of this book? Let's begin with Tim Harper, who edited the manuscript and James Potter, who put the book together at Long Dash Publishing. To my patients who allowed me to enter the deepest sanctums of their minds. To my teachers who taught me. To my friend Tad Frank whose technological knowledge is beyond belief and who was always there to rescue me from technological disaster. To my wife Susan and children Pam and Karen, and stepchildren Meredith and Danielle, who had to put up with years and years of my talking about how I wanted to write. Danielle, my youngest stepdaughter, requires special mention. She taught me Word Perfect, gave me my first computer, typed all my work, was always available, any hour of the day or night, to tell me what to do when I messed up the manuscript, and put up with a lot of grumpiness in the process. So at the risk of creating some sibling rivalry, I have no choice but to dedicate this book to you, Danielle, with loving gratitude. Lastly, I want to thank my mother Pescle, father William, brothers George and Israel, and Uncle Yankle, all of whom are up in Heaven looking down on all this. I hope you approve.

Samuel T. Shein, Ph.D.   *March 2006*
Mind-Body Wellness Institute
757 Teaneck Road
Teaneck NJ 07666

Table of Contents

Part I Psychological Awareness

Part II Communication

Part III Problem Solving and Conflict Resolution

Part I

Psychological Awareness

The first strategy in solving any personal or emotional problem is becoming Psychologically Aware of the issues at hand. This first section on developing Psychological Awareness is intended to give us the insights necessary to develop Strategies for Everyday, thereby developing the Psychological Edge.

CHAPTER 1

The Challenges of Everyday Living

Day to day can be a difficult proposition. The tensions and frustrations we encounter are overwhelming. We need something to help us cope. Some people rely on tranquilizers or "good mood" drugs, but there are other, healthier ways to learn to deal with everyday life. We need to arm ourselves with as many psychological mechanisms as we can. Those psychological mechanisms can provide us with the insights that help us develop Strategies For Everyday Living and ultimately give us The Psychological Edge – the advantage that sound psychology brings to us.

If we look at contemporary society, we see a rather interesting phenomenon. Although people can be successful in their professional or occupational life, they can be dismal failures in their personal lives. We see smart people acting dumb. Sophisticated people acting dumb. Professionally successful people acting dumb. Somehow when it comes time to handle our personal lives, too many of us seem to fall short of the mark.

As one professionally successful songwriter-entertainer put it in a documentary describing his life: "I have had an extraordinary life... A wonderful life... A successful life... Success beyond what I or anyone else could imagine... I have had everything I or anyone else could imagine... I have had everything in my lifetime... Everything except in one area... In the area of my personal life... Things just did not turn out... Not in the way I would have liked them to turn out." So often the personal happiness we so desperately seek eludes us.

What is it that stops us from attaining that success in our personal lives? That lasting feeling of happiness? Why is it that we can be bright, talented, successful and still fail in our personal lives? Our marriages fall apart. Our children grow up emotionally crippled. Why can we be so loved and respected in our business or professional careers, yet such dismal failures in our personal lives?

In many cases, our failures are due to a lack of knowledge, a lack of insight. Putting it bluntly, not many of us know what we are doing when it comes to our personal lives. We know very little about our own human psyche. And even less about the human psyches of other people. Whatever we do know, more often than not, was picked up or learned more by chance than through any formal education or thoughtful pursuit of insight. In fact, no one ever taught us how to understand other people or ourselves. No one ever taught us how to handle ourselves in our daily lives. Sure, we were given golden rules to follow: "Do unto others as you would have them do unto you." Or: "You get more out of people with sugar than vinegar." But no one spoke to us about how we felt, or gave us any insight into the world of psychological strategies for everyday living. In fact, most of us remember the saying "children should be seen and not heard" more often than recalling any sage insights into effective interpersonal living.

So how should we know very much about human nature if it was never taught to us and was never made available to us through any formal training? Of course, in recent years some private educational programs have become available, but there have been very limited attempts at introducing practical psychological courses into our public and private schools. Consequently, it's up to us ourselves, on our own, to acquire the skills necessary to become successful in our personal lives.

Developing skills of any sort requires the investment of a great deal of time, energy and hard work. How much time, energy and hard work have we invested in our efforts to become successful in our personal lives? The answer is: Not Much

We spend years educating ourselves to be successful in our chosen occupations or professions, yet we spend very little time preparing ourselves for handling the rigors of everyday living. We never learned, or had the opportunity to learn, about the psychological concepts and psychological strategies that could help us live happy, successful lives. Instead, we grew up with very little understanding of ourselves, other people, or the knowledge of how to put it all together. Yet, without adequate preparation, we expect to be successful in our interpersonal relationships, i.e. in our dating, marriages, work relationships, and intimate relationships.

Just think of it. We spend years educating ourselves to prepare for successful careers, yet we have virtually no education or preparation for handling our personal lives. Would an engineer ever think of tackling an engineering career without years of study? Would a lawyer or doctor ever think of handling a tough case without proper consultation, study and preparation? Yet that same engineer, lawyer, or doctor will jump right into a marriage, family, or intimate relationship without having the foggiest idea as to how to make those relationships work. Is there any wonder that smart people do act dumb and often end up grossly unsuccessful in our personal lives?

We are born totally helpless. We cannot talk, walk, or take care of ourselves. From that helpless, vulnerable state we are expected to grow up to be strong, healthy, achieving adults. Just how it happens is really left to happenstance more than to anything else. Looking back to our early childhood training, we see that our own parents knew very little about child psychology or how to go about raising mentally healthy adults.

In school, where we were all mandated to attend at least until the age of sixteen, we were exposed year after year to intellectual education. We learned how to read, write and do arithmetic. Yet no one paid very much attention to our psyches, the other part of our minds, the non-intellectual part. Most of the time our teachers paid little attention to our inner feeling and turmoil that pervaded our very existence everyday we entered school. Why should they, no one ever taught them about feelings and what to do about them?

Thinking back to childhood, how many of us can remember anyone, teachers or parents or any other adults, taking time out to ask us how we felt inside, or what we were thinking about in those small heads of ours? Had someone paid attention to the inner workings of the minds of our children, perhaps we would have fewer minds pushing their way into schoolyard shootings, fewer serial rapists and killers, and fewer deranged minds slipping through the cracks of discovery. It was almost as if no one noticed those troubled psyches on the way to disaster. It is interesting to note that while we have a National Transportation Safety Board (NTSB) to investigate train derailings and plane crashes, we do not have a National Psychological Research Board (NPRB) that could investigate national disasters created by people crashing or going off the rails. Is it not important for all of us to know what caused children to bring guns to school to kill other children? How else can we work to prevent that from happening again in our own backyards?

So you want to become successful in life. And you want to develop the psychological edge. How do you go about achieving it? How do you teach it to your children and your families? Over the past 40 years, I have had the distinct privilege of having been allowed into the intimate lives of thousands of patients. In a sense, I have spent the last 40 years of my life behind the couch helping people put their lives together. Success in life is always a goal in psychotherapy and hence I have had ample opportunity to observe quite closely what it takes to create a successful life. For me, success in life requires three basic elements: (1) Psychological Awareness, (2) Communication, and (3) a meaningful Problem Solving/Conflict Resolution approach to everyday living.

While my patients have ranged in age from three years old to ninety years old, invariably the solution to their problems rested in those three areas. Yet it is interesting to note that nowhere in contemporary society do we find any institution, center of higher learning, or individual researchers focusing their attention on facilitating the learning of these skills for our children, our families, and ourselves. Some attempts are currently being made to teach our children a piece of these three elements, and while I have been actively involved in participating in such projects, there still is no widespread understanding by the public at large as to how important psychological awareness, communication, and effective problem-solving techniques are in making us successful in everyday living. To the contrary, there are many people who still block out knowing anything psychological. They refer to important, often crucial information as "psychobabble," thereby diminishing and disdaining what ought to be taken as invaluable information: information that could make us more insightful and hence successful in tackling the difficult task of everyday living. The days should be long behind us when people had to sneak into their psychotherapist's office in order not to be seen.

By this point in time, we should all understand that psychology and psychotherapy are there to help us learn more about ourselves and other people, and how to use what we've learned. Judging from how few people find it easy to handle the rigors and stresses in everyday life, we all could use as much extra help as is possibly available.

Another point that is important here is to understand that throughout the years there have been many different approaches in psychology, with each approach focusing on the theoretical issue of psychological maladjustment rather than on what it takes for a person to be successful in life. Achieving The Psychological Edge focuses more on daily living and what we have to do to make that day happier and more successful. There are many things that we needed to learn that no one ever taught us. Mostly, one learns these things in psychotherapy when we are fortunate enough to have a good psychotherapy teacher. Most people do not realize that psychotherapy is an educational-learning procedure and not a medical procedure. When I do marriage counseling, for instance, I am teaching couples about themselves, about the other person in the relationship, and about strategies on how to put things together. It is entirely a learning experience. It is like going to a special school to learn about human nature, a kind of postgraduate course in human relationships.

While we were never taught the necessary skills that we needed to learn in order to be happy and successful in life, those skills were being taught in psychotherapy. So we had a chance of learning them, albeit in a rather round about way, by seeking assistance with our mental health problems. Unfortunately, even that area of access to those special skills is now being blocked and taken away from us by the so-called "managed care" structure in our healthcare system. At best most people are allowed on an average no more than 10 to 12 maximum sessions of psychotherapy, hardly enough time to solve our mental health problems let alone time to learn new skills. So where do we go to learn these skills? And just what are these new skills? And how will they help people become happier and more successful in life?

To begin with, no one ever taught us who we are. What is the psychological composition of a human being, a person like you and me? We do not know who we are, or even how to go about learning who we are and what people, both ourselves and others, are like. I would suspect that at some point in the not too distant future we will have to go to the Web to learn those things. But for the time being, I would hope that the pages that follow will provide some guidelines that would help us manage our daily lives a bit more easily and a bit more effectively.

Beginning with an explanation of who we are, the following pages guide us to an understanding of such areas as: How psychological symptoms are developed; What the major emotions are and how to handle them; Understanding the secret ingredient in mental health and how to develop it in yourself and your family; Developing a working relationship within yourself and with others that will make life more satisfying; Looking at intimacy and sexuality in a different way; Developing different ways that you can use personally to reduce the stress of everyday living; and most of all, Becoming the kind of person you yourself would like to be.

So let's begin the journey into Psychological Awareness, Communication, and Problem-Solving as it pertains to our everyday living.

CHAPTER 2

Understanding Ourselves: Who Am I?

We all encounter frustration in our daily living. Yet, most of us, myself included, have a rather difficult time understanding where that frustration comes from. One major source of this everyday frustration comes from not knowing who we are and how we operate. More often than not, our perception of who and what we are is far removed from reality. Furthermore, very few of us understand what the basic component of the human psyche looks like.

In order to deal effectively with the frustrations of everyday living, we have to know who we are. Knowing who I am then allows me to understand what I need. It focuses me and gives me direction. It allows me to undo the frustration, or it helps me to stop it from happening. So the question of who I am becomes extremely important in unraveling, minimizing, and controlling our daily frustrations. Knowing who I am brings me in direct contact with what I need in order to negotiate effectively that day. It also brings me in contact with an understanding of what is going wrong, thereby providing me with an opportunity to FEEL better, THINK differently about the situation, or BEHAVE differently. Knowing who I am allows me latitude within which to operate.

So who am I? Basically I am composed of three parts. I have one outside part and two inside parts. My outside part is my outer BEHAVIOR and my two inside parts are my inner FEELINGS and my inner THINKING. So, as a human being I go through life behaving, feeling and thinking.

In the course of growing up we become unbalanced. Some of us, because of our upbringing or early childhood experiences, tend to emphasize one part of the triad more than another. For instance, while growing up, if my family tended not to show much emotion and did not communicate with each other and we just did not talk about how we felt or what we thought, I most probably would have grown up just going through life doing (Behaving) without thinking too much about it and not focusing on what I was feeling about it either:

Type 1 → Behavior Dominates Functioning

However, if I grew up in a family where there was a great deal of emotion expressed in the family or I was exposed to an emotional laden environment I might have grown up unbalanced emotionally:

Type 2 → Feelings Dominate Functioning

Lastly, if I grew up in a rather logical, cognitive environment where rationality was coveted over raw emotion, I then would most probably have grown up to become an unbalanced, rationally oriented adult:

Type 3 → Thinking Dominates Functioning

Just what does all this mean? It means that not knowing who I am in terms of my psychological makeup makes it extremely difficult to understand why I am unhappy with people, not getting along with people, or just plain frustrated in my everyday living. Perhaps a specific example or two will help clarify the issue. Several years ago, I began seeing a middle-aged man in psychotherapy. His chief complaint, the reason he sought therapy, was because of a depression that he recently was experiencing. As we began to talk about when his depression began it became apparent to me that his depression was related to his work and that the real reason he was depressed was because he could not get along with his boss. As I listened to his description of his boss it became quite clear to me that his boss was a cognitive, Type 3 person. It was equally clear that my patient was a very feeling sort of person, a Type 2 person. My patient needed to have his feeling recognized in the workplace. He needed his boss to compliment him on the job he was doing and to be gentle with his criticism, just the way my patient was doing with hundreds of employees he had under him. Since my patient was second in command, he reasoned that his boss, the overall head of the organization, should be able to be decent, respectful, and appreciative. To the contrary, the big boss was a cognitive, rational, unfeeling guy who expected the second in command not to need that kind of attention. Because he liked my patient very much he purposely did not compliment him in order to toughen him up. So what we had was a battle between a feeling person working with and for a cognitive superior. Although my patient's depression lifted once he understood that his boss really liked him and there was nothing personal in his boss's attitude toward him, he could not live with the situation as it stood. In all probability his boss, as a Type 3, cognitively functioning human being, would continue to be unfeeling in his behavior toward my patient. Therefore, my patient resigned and found employment with a family-controlled firm where feelings meant more than cognitive functioning. Some months later, his wife called to settle his bill. She told me he was very happy. Pinned up on the wall of her husband's new office, she told me, was a diagram that I had drawn for him in my office showing the three states of human functioning: Thinking, Feeling, Behavior. He never wanted to forget what he had learned.

When I see patients in my office, I always think of that person or couple in terms of their *behavior – feelings – thinking* triad. When I cannot reach a person in a dialogue, invariably I am not communicating in their triad. Feeling people need to be communicated to on a feeling level and cognitive people need to be talked to on a rational plane. People who are not interested in either feelings or thinking need to be told the bare essential facts and nothing more.

When I see children in psychotherapy who want something from their parents such as a bicycle, I usually say to them: If your mother is the feeling one in your family tell her, "Mom, if I get a bike I will be so happy and overjoyed...I can't tell you how wonderful I will feel." And if your father is the rational one in the family, tell him, "Dad, if I get a bike I will be able to ride myself to school and mom won't have to drive me...I could do errands for people by going to the store for them, and for Mom too." The major strategy here is to become aware of your own Behavior - Thinking - Feeling triad. Do you favor one area over another? Do you come from a family that favors one area of functioning over another? Are you like them? Or are you different? Are you content with who you are? What would you like to change? Do you get frustrated with people who are Type 1, 2, or 3? Which type or types do you like and dislike? Can you improve your effectiveness with people by recognizing which type they are and communicate with them on that level?

If you are a Type 1 person you do not want to hear all those details. You just want to get things done. You do not want to waste your time thinking about things or worrying about feelings, you just want to complete the task.

If you are a Type 2 person, you are more concerned with the feeling aspect of the task. How will people feel about the situation? You will care more about the people and their feelings rather than the speed with which the task can be completed, or the right and correct approach to the activity.

If you are a Type 3 person, you want to understand the situation rationally. How does this all fit together and what is the right way to do the task? This is the way it ought to be done, carefully and correctly.

Who are you? Identify yourself and pay special attention to the triad of Behavior – Thinking – Feeling as you go about your daily routine. Check it out. See if these concepts can help you locate and reduce the frustration in your daily routine.

So in your day to day dealings with people pay special attention to your own psychological makeup as well as to theirs. Develop your own psychological edge.

CHAPTER 3

Understanding Others: Who Are You?

If I am composed of three parts (Behavior, Thinking and Feelings), then it stands to reason that you too are composed of the same three elements. In any discussion, then, we have six issues that we can talk about: My feelings, thinking or behavior; or your feelings, thinking or behavior. Too often, I assume that your Behavior, Thinking and Feelings are proportionate to mine. If my Feelings are dominant on any particular issue, I tend to assume that your Feelings – rather than your Thinking, for example, are dominant for you, too. But that's often not the case, of course.

Me (My Triad)	You (Your Triad)
1. Behavior	4. Behavior
2. Feelings	5. Feelings
3. Thinking	6. Thinking

Invariably, when we interact with each other, or just talk to each other, we rarely realize where we are, i.e., in which triad we are operating. Now why is it so important to know in which triad we are operating? Basically because when we become FRUSTRATED with each other it helps a great deal to know how that frustration developed. For instance, I may be very annoyed with my friend Jay. Unless I realize he is constantly talking about his own way of THINKING (#6), I may not have a clear way of fixing it. Instead, my solution may be just to avoid him. In so doing I may continue to be frustrated and stew inside of myself. We all know how unhealthy that is. To avoid people is to leave us alone and lonely, an equally unhealthy state of affairs. Visualizing the triad, allows us to realize that the frustration is coming directly from our inability to get back to our side of the continuum so that we can talk about our own feelings (#2) or way of thinking (#3). In any discussion, understanding that two triads exist helps us focus our attention and can give us a sense of balance and control in interpersonal situations. It allows us to focus on the other person when we are so inclined, like when we are uncomfortable with the discussion but do not know how to shift the discussion or where to go with it. It allows us to focus on what we need in the discussion. When conversations get bogged down it allows us to focus the discussion making life less boring and uninteresting.

Young people in therapy often ask me about how to keep a discussion going, often feeling uncomfortable with the lulls in conversations. Keeping in mind that there are six areas of discussion possible can help alleviate that anxiety. Disagreements in discussions quite often are due to the fact that one person is talking about feelings when the other person is talking about taking a purely behavioral or non-feeling approach to the problem at hand.

Balance and control are two important concepts in psychology because they give us a way to maintain our sense of inner harmony, our sense of inner peace. Not knowing where we are in a dialogue gives us that uncomfortable feeling of uneasiness, whereas knowing where we are or where we might want to go in the discussion makes us not only feel relaxed, it also gives us a good feeling about ourselves and makes us feel powerful.

When I see patients in my office, I usually pay a great deal of attention to the flow of the communication, noting which side of the continuum we are on, mine or theirs, as well as to the content of the discussion as to whether it is cognitive, feeling or just behavioral. That gives me a clue as to where the other person is at and how I might approach them to get my point across to them. Not too long ago I began to speak to the mother of an 8-year-old child I was seeing in psychotherapy. I began to notice that every time I spoke about things on my side of the continuum the discussion shifted to her side of the continuum. Focusing on that shifting, I further observed that she had to qualify everything that I was saying. Paying even closer attention to where she was going with our discussion showed me that I had better say everything perfectly otherwise we were back on her side of the continuum correcting me. I waited until I was certain of my discovery and then said to the woman, who was a very likeable person: "Please don't be offended by what I am about to say, but you scare me. It seems if I am not perfect in what I say to you, you won't like me. You scare me." Several weeks later, she came in to chat about her daughter again and told me that her child's teacher had told her that her daughter was trying to be too perfect. She then said," You know what you told me about how I scared you because I need things to be too perfect? Well, I think you are right. I am going to have to work on that."

CHAPTER 4

The Defensiveness of the Ego

Everyone knows when our immune system is impaired, serious physical illnesses develop such as AIDS. Namely, that our bodies have a defensive structure that protects us. But what most people do not know is that the mind, like the body, also has a defensive structure that protects us mentally. Sigmund Freud made that rather brilliant discovery in the early nineteen hundreds. Freud originally identified some thirteen mechanisms of defense. Modern textbooks in psychology cite eight mechanisms of defense: Repression; Projection; Reaction Formation; Displacement; Intellectualization; Rationalization; Denial; and Sublimation.

These defense mechanisms protect our egos from being hurt. Like the mechanisms that protect the body, they tend to become harmful to us under certain conditions and at certain times. For instance, when surgeons want to do a heart, or liver, transplant our bodies reject that heart or liver as being foreign to that body. Consequently, special medications need to be administered to the patient in order to nullify the organ's rejection, to nullify the body's defensive system. In a similar way, the mind's defensive structure interferes with our being able to accept criticism, a rather important trait when it comes to getting along with each other, or just correcting the mistakes we make in everyday living. Unfortunately, unlike modern medicine, psychologists have not come up with a special medication or formula by which to nullify the defensiveness of our egos. We desperately need one.

In light of the absence of an ego anti-defensive mechanism, it becomes very important for each one of us to recognize that getting along with each other requires a great deal of give and take. In order to accomplish that goal in everyday living we have to nullify our defensive structure by first realizing its very existence, and second by taking definitive steps not to just focus on our issues, but to look very closely at what others are saying negatively about us. Over the years I have given this procedure of looking very closely to the criticalness of others various names such as Decoding and SDP, or Self-Directed Psychology. SDP, Self-Directed Psychology, means that in any conflict situation that we find ourselves in should result in our first taking a look at what we ourselves contributed negatively to the conflict situation before we conclude that it's all the other person's fault. The defensive nature of our egos will usually find some reason to blame the other person rather than ourselves. In so doing, we are unable to decode, and truly understand, what is really taking place

Putting it another way, when people are critical of us we should pay special attention to that criticalness because it can become a time of great learning. We can learn how others see us and we can decode it in terms of developing greater insight into ourselves, and the world around us. Without criticism we may not grow and develop that potential we all have within us.

Having consulted with school systems for many years, and having raised four daughters as well as having grown up in a family of three boys, I can tell you from first hand experience how important it is to really listen to the negative feedback that teachers and school personnel offer parents. The negative feedback is far more valuable than the positive feedback. Too often we hear the much over used phrase "Not my child!" Negative feedback about our children allows us to make adjustments in how we are raising them thereby warding off disasters in later life.

I can recall a school guidance counselor telling a parent that her son was paling around with, and using marijuana with, a group of rebellious students. The mother was irate and came to me to bitterly complain. How could the guidance counselor say these mean things about her son? Several years after the boy graduated from high school, I ran into the woman and inquired as to how her son was doing. She told me that he was recently released from a drug rehab center. When I expressed my regret over her difficulty with her son she replied: "This is his third drug rehab placement...I should have listened to that guidance counselor five years ago...It would have saved me a lot of heart ache."

On another level, I can recall seeing a couple in psychotherapy several years ago. This was his third marriage and all his wives had the same complaint. He gave so much to his job that there was nothing left for them or his children. It took three marriages and some intensive psychotherapy to finally get through to him. He finally got it. How many of us just don't get it! It's those darn defense mechanisms that are at the root of much of our not getting it.

Before going on, I think it is important that we take a look at just what these defense mechanisms are all about:

Repression - The automatic process of keeping unacceptable communications (thoughts and feelings) from conscious awareness. While it is like forgetting, there is a high price we pay for using this mechanism. It requires an enormous expenditure of energy, often compared to the energy required to hold a beach ball under water. Have you ever felt you just didn't have enough energy to go on? Perhaps the repression mechanism was being overly used?

Projection - The process of seeing those unacceptable traits, behaviors, feelings in others that are really our own. Psychology graduate students in my time were notorious for using this concept on each other. Whenever you called another grad student on a critical point, they would usually deny it and tell you "You're projecting," thereby escaping the criticism and putting the blame on you.

Reaction Formation - When one's Behavior is unconsciously opposite to what we really think or feel, we are engaging in reaction formation behavior. When I was in psychoanalytic training many years ago, I recall hearing about a man who was on a crusade to close down gay bars. The sad result was that many of the gay people in the community had no place to go to socialize, which resulted in social isolation and hospitalized breakdowns. With the hospitals becoming filled, several of the senior members of the mental health community looked into the problem only to find that the man who was leading the fight against the homosexual community was himself most probably gay. By fighting the battle against the gay community he could deny his own homosexuality.

Displacement - Taking our feelings out onto other people, places, or things is common behavior we all engage in. The cartoon where the wife nags the husband who promptly kicks the dog immediately comes to mind. I can recall an incident when I was a young psychology intern being reprimanded by the chief psychologist for not giving a complete Rorschach (the inkblot test) and turning my fury on another intern who interrupted us to ask if he could borrow my stopwatch.

Intellectualization - When we de-emotionalize an event or activity and treat it in a colder, abstract manner we are intellectualizing. Perhaps most common is when we proclaim that it does not bother us when the person we are dating has many other suitors, saying things like "Competition never hurt anyone."

Rationalization - Giving a good excuse for the real reason constitutes rationalization. "I really was too tired to go for that job interview" rather than the truth, "I didn't go on that job interview because I was too intimidated by the kind of interview they give" is an example of rationalization.

Denial - Most of us use denial a great deal of the time. "I certainly did not do that...It's all in your mind" are quite common in our everyday functioning. Unfortunately, it prevents us from ever correcting our faults if we keep denying them and don't "fess up."

Sublimation - Of all the defense mechanisms, sublimation is the most benign. It occurs when we convert our personal, individual needs into socially acceptable needs. Hence, I may have a strong need for power and dominance. By becoming a successful surgeon who volunteers much of his or her time to helping underprivileged patients obtain the surgical procedures they require, I have sublimated my personal need for power into an activity that will bring me that power, but it will also benefit society. We need more people in society sublimating their needs.

Before leaving this topic, it is important to remember that getting along with people means being able to listen to them so that we understand where they are coming from. Good mental health means listening to what others have to say. It is also a good practice if you ever expect to have successful business or good personal relationships. In order to do so, you have to find a way to nullify your own defensive structure. Work on it. It may be one of the most important things you ever do for yourself, or your family. Living with people who are less defensive tends to make life a bit easier and more pleasant, something we can all appreciate.

CHAPTER 5

What Exactly Is Good Mental Health?

When Freud was asked how he would define good mental health, he usually replied that a person is in good mental health when they are "happy in love and in work." What he was undoubtedly referring to is that people are generally in good shape when they are happy in their personal lives and in the workplace, two major areas of our existence. If Freud were alive today, I am equally certain that he would amplify and add to his definition of what he considered to be good mental health.

If we are to achieve the psychological edge, and have successful strategies for everyday living, we must have a clear understanding and a good working relationship with what it takes to develop good mental health. My own concept of what constitutes good mental health comes from working in therapy over the last 40 years with children, adolescents, adults, families, and couples. It is based on a communication model.

In my view of things, a person is in good mental health when they: 1. Know what they are feeling and thinking. 2. Can communicate those feelings and thoughts to other people. 3. Can receive the feelings and thinking communication from other people. Hence, good mental health involves having an effective internal feedback communication (IFC) system between me and me; a good external feedback communication (EFC) system, which allows us to effectively communicate with others; and an effective outside feedback communication (OFC) system, which allows us to effectively receive communication from others. This is how it should work.

If I am in a social situation, say a social gathering of friends and someone insults me, I need to react or not react to that insult by being aware of what I am feeling and or thinking. It is my feelings and or my thinking that shapes my reaction, my behavior. If I were not in touch with either my feelings or thinking, then I really would not know how to behave, or what to do. I need to react to that insult so I have to depend on my feelings and thinking to help me decide what to do. Most probably I would feel hurt and angry, and I might think that the person who insulted me was a jerk. At that point I may act or choose not to take any action, depending upon how intense my feelings were and how seriously I was thinking about the situation. At any rate, unless my feelings and thoughts register within me, i.e., if I am not tuned into myself, I am in trouble psychologically because my behavior may not reflect what is going on in the situation (reality). Hence, I would be behaving inappropriately, inappropriate to what the situation calls for. When we behave inappropriately, that behavior could mark us as a person who is a jerk, a wimp, stupid, or just plain weird.

When I was a psychology intern, I walked onto the psychiatric floor of the hospital one day to find Mary, a 45-year-old patient, dancing on a tabletop. I asked her what was going on, to which she replied, "I'm having fun... I'm celebrating... my mother just died." Mary was Psychotic. She had no idea what she was experiencing inside of herself. She was totally out of touch with her feelings and her thinking. She was behaving in a totally inappropriate manner, in this case behaving psychotically. Her IFC, internal feedback system, was totally inoperative.

At a less severe level, I would like to tell you about Benjamin, a 51-year-old tool designer who had worked for the same firm for over 20 years. When he wanted to leave the firm about 14 years ago, the owner of the firm asked him to stay on and promised him a partnership in the firm when he the owner retired.

Since it turned out to be that the owner retired some 5 years ago, the group therapy members inquired as to what happened to the partnership offer, to which Benjamin replied: "I just never got around to asking about it." Benjamin was sent into therapy by his wife, whose chief complaint was that living with Benjamin was like living alone. He just did not react to life. She said he was more like a zombie than a real live human being. Because of Benjamin's background, his early childhood years, he learned not to tune into his inner feelings and thoughts. It would have been too dangerous then. So what happened is that Benjamin grew up having a defective IFC, and therapy was geared to helping him develop in adulthood what he deliberately was forced not to do in childhood, have a good operating internal feedback communication (IFC) system.

Knowing what we feel and think is crucial in helping us negotiate everyday living. Without such knowledge we are left helpless and possibly hopeless. That is exactly what Freud was after when he taught us all "to make conscious what is unconscious." Not knowing what we feel and think results in our paying a rather high price. As we will see in the next chapter, when we are not tuned into what is going on in us we are open and vulnerable to developing psychological and even physical symptoms. Recent studies have even pinpointed the problem more precisely. Unconscious anger and hostility is being linked more and more to the development of physiological changes in the body which affect our immune system and may be underlying such conditions as heart disease, cancer, diabetes, pain and other physical illnesses.

At any rate, people are mentally healthy when they know what they feel and think, can communicate those feelings and thoughts to other people, and can receive the feelings and thoughts of other people. If we want to be mentally healthy we must pursue those three goals in our everyday living.

CHAPTER 6

How Symptoms Are Developed

One of the most important pieces of information a person can have is understanding about how psychological (and at times physical) symptoms are developed. Once again we see that no one ever taught us how symptoms are developed. Yet, it would be so very important to have this knowledge at our disposal so that we can work diligently to prevent ourselves and our families from developing unhealthy patterns of behavior which in turn could lead us into developing psychologically induced headaches, stomach ailments, anxieties, depressions, rages, withdrawals, addictions, somatizations, and the like. Yes, it is possible to prevent most of these psychologically induced symptoms from developing. This is how it works.

When we were young children, say from birth through 2, 3, and 4 years of age, we expressed quite directly what we felt and what we thought. A 2-year-old will hit you and take your ball away from you because h/she just wants it. That is good mental health in the sense that what is inside of us is being expressed directly outside of us. The inside matches the outside. So far so good. But as we all know, the child cannot continue to act that way. The parents and their surrogates begin to teach this child that h/she cannot continue to act this way for a variety of reasons including the fact that other people will be hurt by such behavior and that no one will like us if we continue to act that way. Hence, the child begins to develop what I call a psychological THERMOSTAT to control what is going on inside versus what is being expressed on the outside. If this THERMOSTAT becomes overloaded, it can malfunction. We may express ourselves in ways that are inappropriate, or not in our own interests. We may hurt others, directly or indirectly, and we may hurt ourselves, too.

Maturity helps us develop our thermostat. But adulthood also brings more responsibility – and the stresses that go with responsibility. Our THERMOSTATS can become so clogged that what is inside pushes to get outside only to find that the one way to get outside is to go around the barrier, much like a river overflowing a dam, thereby creating symptoms:

Derivative Expressions (Symptoms)

1. Headaches   5. Rages
2. Stomach   6. Withdrawals
3. Anxiety   7. Addiction
4. Depression   8. Somatization

The key here is to have achieved the optimum opening in our thermostats. Unfortunately, not too many of us know about having thermostats, let alone concentrating on how to regulate them.

In the course of psychotherapy, symptoms are decreased or are removed entirely depending upon the severity of the symptom. All of this is generally accomplished without the use of medication, a rather important factor to remember. Symptoms can be removed by talking about them, thereby opening the barrier (thermostat) that keeps the conflict hidden. Once the conflict is removed, the symptom should lessen. The trick is to be able to name the conflict. Let's see if I can give a clear-cut example of it.

As a young psychologist, just as I was entering my postgraduate training in Psychoanalysis, I began treating a young woman who was going through a tough period in her life. She suffered from intense feelings of anxiety and depression. Because of the intensity of her psychological anguish, I would see her several times a week. I felt quite comfortable with her, and she with me because I had seen her in therapy when she was a teenager and I was an intern, some five years earlier. I had helped her then and fully expected to help her now. One day I received an emergency call from her mother, Katherine was totally debilitated. The anxiety and depression were destroying her. She could not eat, sleep, or even stand by herself without being supported. Could I possibly see her today? Of course I did.

Katherine was brought into my office by her mother. She could hardly walk. She was so weak that she could hardly sit and had to use my analytic couch to rest on. Because of the severity of her symptoms we did our psychotherapy work with Katherine sitting up. This time she really was experiencing the full brunt of her symptoms. As I inquired as to what had happened, Katherine related that she was having terrible nightmares that were terrorizing her. She dreamed that she was caught in a terrible fire that burned and destroyed her house, her furniture, and all her possessions. Everything around her was charred, burnt and smoldering. She kept having the same or similar dreams night after night until she began to believe that her house was about to actually burn down. She felt tortured by the fact that she saw herself night after night in the middle of this fire, her dress burned and her face and body blackened by the fire.

All my attempts at uncovering what the dream meant failed. In as much as there was so much destruction in the dream, I probed the possibility that Katherine was harboring (repressing) strong feelings of hurt, anger, and rage. But we could not find anyone with whom Katherine was angry. Was she angry with me, her therapist? "No." Her parents? "No." Her siblings? "No." With anyone in the recent past? "No...not anyone." My recent analytic training had taught me that Freud always spoke of two basic drives, the aggressive drive and the sexual drive. I was certain that Katherine, a very warm and loving youngster, had a great deal of difficulty, as so many of us do, with confronting people, and that her blocked aggressive drive was behind her anxiety and depression. Yet, all my attempts at leading her in the aggressive arena failed. She did not connect her nightmares to anything aggressive. What was left for us to explore? Of course, the sexual sphere. Katherine had never dealt with her sexuality in any previous session. She was very shy about her aggressive fantasies so I knew she would be very uncomfortable talking about sex. Nevertheless, I began, "Could your dream have anything to do with something sexual?" She did not answer. Not knowing whether she heard me I repeated the question. This time she replied, "Yes." I then asked her to explain the connection that she saw between her dream and something sexual. She refused. Instead, she said, "You'll have to ask me some more questions." I began, "Does this sexual thing have to do with you?" She replied, "Yes." "Is it something you read?" "No." "Is it something you saw in a magazine?" "No." "Is it something you saw on TV?" "No." "What is it?" "You'll have to keep asking me questions." So, I continued, "Is this something you felt?" "Yes." "You're having sexual feelings?" "Yes." "That's it, you're having sexual feelings?" "Yes, but there is more to it." "So tell me the rest of it." "You'll have to keep asking me more questions." "Are you having sexual feelings about someone in particular?" "Yes." "Who?" Silence followed by "Keep asking me questions." "OK." "Is the person in the state where we live?" "Yes." "Is the person in the town where you live?" "Yes." "Is the person a neighbor?" "Yes." "You mean you have been having sexual feelings about your neighbor and that has been disturbing you?" "Yes, and you're not mad at me?" "Of course not. You can have any thoughts or feelings about anyone that you want. You can think anything and feel anything without ever feeling guilty or ashamed of it." "Then you're not angry with me?" "Not at all. If anything, I believe your fantasies are entirely normal. Besides, I know that the young man in question is a handsome young fellow your age. No, I'm certainly not angry with you. Nor would I think he would be, either." With that last statement Katherine stood up and said, "I'd like to bring my mother in to see that I'm OK. She's been quite worried about me." In a few seconds, Katherine returned with her mother who kept proclaiming, "It's a miracle. It's a miracle. You gave me my old Katherine back again. You came up with a miracle!"

Of course, it wasn't a miracle, but I never told Katherine's mother it wasn't. I just took credit for it! The important thing is that Katherine and I had come through another crisis together. We were getting the handle on her anxiety and depression. And that felt especially sweet. Hopefully, she would now be free of the guilt and shame that had been paralyzing her, not allowing her to feel and think freely.

The point not to be forgotten here is that identifying underlying issues and communicating about them can help us prevent psychological, and even physical, symptoms from developing. Not communicating is deadly. If you can't talk about things, learn to do so. Otherwise you will suffer the negative consequences of developing psychological and possibly physical symptoms.

CHAPTER 7

Handling Our Emotions: H A D G A S

Many years ago, I began seeing in psychotherapy a series of male patients who would come into their therapy sessions and say something like, "Boy, do I need to be here today," followed by silence. I would respond with, "Good, what would you like to talk about?" which would be followed by further silence. When I prompted these patients to continue, they would invariably say, "I don't know what to talk about...You start me off...What should I talk about?" Usually that led to a typical analytic response of, "You have to initiate the discussion...This is your session and we have to uncover and follow what's inside of you...If I initiate the session perhaps we will be analyzing my unconscious and not yours." This scenario was repeated so many times that I began to sound 'canned,' like I had rehearsed it so many times that it did not sound sincere, or meaningful, or caring. Furthermore, I was boring myself with my own words, and the routine of having to waste the precious, limited time we had to spend together to say these empty words to each other. So I began to think it through. If patients cannot initiate what they need to talk about, don't they have a perfect right to ask their therapists to help them begin the session? Furthermore, who has more experience at this, the patient or the therapist? Still further, the patient is paying for the therapist's expertise, so why not have the therapist earn his or her fee by helping the patient initiate the session?

Therapists are customarily and traditionally taught to allow the patient to initiate sessions and to observe carefully how the patient goes about doing it, thereby obtaining valuable insight into the patient's make-up that then is relayed back to the patient; insight is gained and everyone is happy and content. But what happens if the poor guy sitting there truly can't get started? Again, the training of the therapist is that such non-responsiveness constitutes what is called a resistance, an emotional blockage on the patient's part which requires analysis, which will lead to insight, which will lead to growth, progress and happiness. But what if it just doesn't happen? These patients were drawing blanks. Therefore, I decided to do something about it.

As my patient sat in the chair in front of me in silence, I began to free associate, to answer the questions silently in my own head that I found myself asking my patient. In essence, I began to answer for them silently. What I found was that I continually came up with the same type of material week after week. What happened this week? What frustrations did you go through? Where did you feel HELPLESS? When did you feel ANGRY? Were you DEPRESSED? Did you feel GUILTY? Were you ANXIOUS? Did you experience any feelings of SHAME? Hence, I was asking and answering over and over again about Helplessness, Anger, Depression, Guilt, Anxiety, and Shame. Before long, I began to realize that these six areas were crucial in everyone's life. They were crucial in everyday living. In a sense, these six areas are the psychological pulse of our very existence, just as our blood pulse gives us a readout of our physical health and existence.

This insight provided an immediate gain. We no longer sat around wasting valuable time; sessions became more focused, we made progress faster. In lecturing to single, separated, and divorced groups, something I have been doing for the last ten years, I invariably refer to these six factors in assessing their emotional health. Although technically, helpless may not be considered an emotion, I refer to these six traits as emotions. They are very much states of "being" that play a major role in shaping our daily happiness or unhappiness.

Although managing our emotions is a major task for all of us, the only place in modern civilization where it is taught is in psychotherapy. And, as I have repeatedly pointed out, managed care is rapidly doing away with any form of psychotherapy beyond ten sessions. As I once told a managed care customer service representative, "If I could cure anxiety and depression in ten sessions, I would be in Washington, D.C. and not Teaneck, N.J." So what follows is extremely important because it may be one of the few places that you can learn about your emotions. This is how it works.

Helplessness, Anger, and Depression go together. When I feel helpless, I feel angry and become depressed. I do not want to feel helpless so I become frustrated over the helplessness and I become angry. I may not be aware that I am angry, but you can bet your bottom dollar on the fact that when I feel helpless I do, indeed feel angry. Who would want to feel helpless? Not many of us. The anger, in turn, may not register consciously, and whether it does register consciously or not, it then turns into depression. (I am using depression here to mean unhappiness.) When I myself feel helpless, I sure do not feel happy.

Conversely, when I see a patient who is unhappy, or depressed (either mildly depressed or severely depressed), I work backwards. I look for the hidden helplessness and hidden anger. Quite often the helplessness is more readily visible than the anger. Making the anger conscious and undoing the helplessness usually works wonders for depression. Taking tranquilizers may only mask the anger and helplessness, something we do not want to do. Yet, there certainly are times when taking a tranquilizer aids the process of unmasking the anger and undoing the helplessness. The danger here is that tranquilizers should never be the only way we undo and work out our unhappiness. We do not want to become a nation of people relying on a pill to give us an "up" feeling and another pill to calm us "down." Most managed care companies know that putting a patient on medication is the cheapest way for the companies to escape the real responsibility to the patient − helping that person develop new patterns of coping with anger and helplessness.

Many years ago, I worked with a patient who was depressed for a long, long time, twenty years. Using the H A D concept, we uncovered the anger and identified the helplessness. What had happened is that this person made employment and business decisions that just did not turn out in his favor. Consequently, he harbored a great deal of unconscious anger and hostility toward himself and he felt very helpless because all the decisions that had been made many years ago were affecting him now, and they could not be undone. All of this was unconscious, he was only aware that he was deeply depressed. Medications, vitamin therapy, and all other therapy approaches had failed him for the past twenty years. It was only when I introduced him to the H A D concept did we began to unmask what was taking place in his life. By working out his anger, toward himself and others, and freeing him of the helplessness that he felt, he began to let go of the past and focus on the present. It was then that he finally was able to get rid of the depression that had plagued him for so many years.

With regard to the other three elements in the HADGAS equation, guilt plays an enormous part in our daily living. When we have too much of it, it tends to make us depressed because it also tends to paralyze us and make us feel helpless, thereby contributing to that negative HAD sequence. Insufficient feelings of guilt tend to make us pathological in another way; we end up becoming – or raising – children who are egocentric, self-absorbed, and unfeeling toward others.

Anxiety plays havoc with our daily lives by making us feel uncomfortable in what we are routinely doing. When we feel guilt, we usually feel anxious and uncomfortable. Keeping track of our anxiety as it ebbs and flows up and down can give us a handle on it. Take the man who consulted with a school system on a special project that he worked on once a week. When he realized that he was experiencing anxiety on Friday mornings on his way to work, he brought it to his therapist's attention. The therapist explained it this way, "Inasmuch as you were not at the worksite in a week, we would expect you to be anxious. You do not know what is going on there, what you will do when you arrive there, or how your day will go. Hence, if you can gather some information before you get there and plan your day out, your anxiety could diminish." Sure enough, when our beleaguered consultant planned his day out as he drove to work every Friday morning his anxiety magically disappeared. The principle is simple. At times, to reduce anxiety, structure your day or activity. Become aware of the ebb and flow of your tension and take action. Structuring your activities can reduce anxiety.

Shame is an extremely destructive emotion when it gets out of hand. It can make us feel very uncomfortable and miserable. In a less intense form, shame is not only tolerable; it can be beneficial if its anticipation prevents us from acting in a self-destructive manner. However, generally shame is experienced with its full intensity and hurts us on many different levels, especially doing a great deal of damage to our own self-esteem. Self-esteem is a major issue in our whole scheme of well-being and will be discussed in detail elsewhere. At this juncture, it is important to note that the way we view ourselves and what we feel about ourselves play an enormous role in whether we have inner peace and tranquility in our lives or unrest and tension.

Anyone hoping to live a happy, successful life needs to be aware of helplessness, anger, depression, guilt, anxiety, and shame in their daily lives and must work on finding ways to cope with these emotions. Methods of keeping them in balance are something we turn our attention to next.

Part II

Communication

Communication is the single most important strategy that helps us develop and maintain emotional health and psychological well-being. It is crucial for good self-esteem and essential for us in developing intelligence and success in life.

CHAPTER 8

The Secret Ingredient in Mental Health

In the past 40 years, I have not seen one patient where communication, or the breakdown of communication, was not involved with their problem. Without any hesitancy, I can tell you categorically this: *The secret ingredient in mental health is communication.* Effective communication reduces tension and keeps us mentally and physically healthy. More and more research in the field of mind-body medicine is showing us quite clearly how the mind affects the body and how our minds and bodies are so closely connected.

Perhaps one of the most important lessons to be learned in childhood is that Communication Reduces Tension. When people sit down and talk things out, tension is reduced. Not all of us learned this simple fact of life. Many of us learned that if we speak up tension will be increased not decreased. When we spoke up, we were either criticized, put down, or people just got angry with us. We learned it was not safe to speak up. Hence, many of us go through life keeping things inside of ourselves, but end up paying a high price for it by developing such symptoms as anxiety attacks, depressions, coronary heart disease, phobias, and the like.

In psychotherapy, people come in, sit down, and talk. From that verbal exchange, hundreds of thousand of people around the world report they feel better and their problems seem solved. So why not use the same technique, learning to communicate effectively, to prevent problems from developing in the first place? Over the past several years, I have been working in health psychology, with patients who have serious health problem with pain management, cancer, or coronary heart disease. Just sitting down and talking things out produces a reduction in tension that is readily visible by noticing the reduction in muscle tension in their faces. *Learning how to talk things out is the single most important skill that people need to develop in order to be mentally healthy.*

When I underwent the clinical training in Mind-Body Medicine at the Harvard Medical School in October 1997, Dr. Herbert Benson, the Director of the Mind-Body Medical Institute, told us about a research study that was done at the Massachusetts General Hospital. Prior to surgery, patients were randomly assigned to two groups, an Experimental Group and a Control Group. In the Experimental Group, the anesthesiologist who was assigned to the case came to see the patient the night before the surgery, answered all the patient's questions, sat on the patient's bed, held the patient's hand, and stayed as long as the patient wanted. In the Control Group, the anesthesiologist came to see the patient before surgery, introduced himself, "I am Dr. Brown, I will be your anesthesiologist tomorrow," and left. What was the result of this simple experiment where kindness and communication prevailed? Following surgery, those patients who were in the Experimental Group required 50% less medication and left the hospital 2 to 3 days earlier than those patients in the Control Group. If nothing else, this experiment demonstrates quite clearly the power of positive communication. Communication is Powerful. It can help us or destroy us mentally and even physically.

Our own confidence and self-esteem is very much connected to what we communicate to ourselves. If you think I am wonderful and I contradict that idea by thinking that I am a jerk, the results are low self-esteem and a lack of confidence. Self-esteem is directly related to what I think of me and the messages that I communicate to me about me. For instance, when I am out speaking to singles groups, I often ask them; "How am I doing" ala Mayor Ed Koch. Invariably, I receive loud applause and much adulation. I then turn to the audience and say, "Thank you, that feels great...But if I forgot to tell you about items 3C ~ D, I probably would be very upset with myself, and end up with low self-esteem because I would be critical of myself and communicating negative feedback to myself." When we tell ourselves negative things about ourselves, our confidence and our self-esteem go down the drain. Not many of us understand this connection between internal communication and self-esteem. You can think the world of me, unless I let that positive external communication enter my internal communication system, confidence and self-esteem will not prevail. So once again we can see how important communication, positive communication, is in keeping us mentally healthy.

When we communicate effectively with others, that ability to do so makes us feel good and adds to our confidence and self-esteem because we then send ourselves positive, inter-communication messages. When we do not communicate effectively to others, we may then send ourselves negative, internal communications. The point is that those internal communications, both positive and negative, are responsible for those good or bad feelings we have about ourselves. The strategy here is to monitor those internal communications to ourselves, making them conscious. Once we are aware of them, we have to make the negative ones into positive ones. It goes something like this: After delivering my lecture, I leave. On my way home I begin to realize that I do not feel "up," the way I usually feel after giving my talk. I ponder as to why this is going on, and in this communication within myself I begin to realize that I am feeling a bit "down." Asking myself how come I am feeling down after everything went so well, I come to realize that I forget to tell the audience about items 3C - D. Once I make that discovery, I immediately become annoyed with myself and begin to think and sub-vocally saying negative things about myself, things like, "You jerk you forgot to tell them about 3C – D," and then I proceed to become further angry with myself. My thinking continues to be negative and moves to things like, "Why did this happen?...Can't you get anything right?... What is wrong with you?...How come you do such stupid things?" This negative internal dialogue continues on making me more and more depressed (unhappy) unless I take an active role in controlling and correcting it. Once I am aware of this internal negative dialogue, what I could say to myself is something like, "O.K., I goofed...What can I do about it?...One thing I can do about it is to stop beating myself up over it...How do I do that?...Well, how important is it that they know about it?" If it is not that important, I can say to myself, "They won't even know that I left it out...And besides, they really got a lot out of the lecture and loved it...So why make such a fuss over it...let's chalk that up to experience and not do it again...Or maybe I should do it again, it might have made the lecture less cumbersome (said with internal laughter)."

If I come to the conclusion that I left several major points out of the lecture, I could do one of several things to correct the omission. I could contact the group and ask their leader to make the points for me at their next gathering, or I could draft a letter to the group making those points that I left out. The letter could either be read to the group or a copy of the letter could be sent or distributed to the group at the next meeting. I then could communicate to myself something like, "Boy, do I feel so much better now that I handled that problem...I feel so relaxed I think that I'm going to sleep very well tonight... I am feeling very good."

By turning negative internal communication to positive internal communication, through my internal conflict resolution dialogue, I have gone from a negative mental health state to a positive mental health state. The secret ingredient in mental health is Communication.

In a very similar way, if I do not know what to say to people, why on earth should I not be shy, insecure, and feel inferior. If you have not gotten the message yet, here it is: Communication is the secret ingredient in mental health.

Perhaps one of the best examples of how communication is so intricately interwoven with mental health occurred in the treatment of a 16-year-old boy. It was my first private patient. Previously, I had spent the past four years treating children, adolescents, adults, and families at the one major mental health facility in the area, the county hospital mental health center. I was very anxious to develop a private practice and to be out on my own. My first referral was a bright, wonderful young man, a high school sophomore. He was depressed and his high school counselor, who knew me quite well, thought we would be a good match and referred the family to me. My first approach to Jay was to establish a friendship within which we could work effectively together to resolve his problem, the sadness emanating from his depression. Although Jay and I became close friends, and he trusted me by revealing his inner most feelings and desires, we just could not get Jay to really be happy. Psychologists generally do not suggest that their patients go on medication, and that was the case with Jay, especially being a 16-year-old. Psychologists do very well with their patients figuring out what is causing the problem, then developing a plan to correct it. But all of this was not working with Jay. No matter how well the session went, Jay would return next week depressed. What to do about it?

Reviewing Jay's therapy sessions, I began to understand what was happening and why his parents were pulling their hair out. Jay was doing a terrible number on himself. Although all of us felt that Jay was doing very well, he did not think so. He wanted to be "popular." That meant very popular. Visibly popular to himself. In his eyes he was not "really" popular. No matter what, Jay was not going to let up on himself until he became popular. Unraveling the popularity issue and discovering how terribly important and connected to Jay's depression it was took a long time to uncover (what Freud called making conscious what is unconscious). So we began to work on becoming popular to Jay's satisfaction.

In as much as we had worked on Jay's thinking, and that was not sufficient to bring about a change to satisfy Jay, and the depression continued, I thought we ought to turn to Jay's behavior. Remembering that there are three parts to a person, Behavior, Thinking and Feelings, and when one area is in trouble, you basically have the other two to work with; I began to question Jay about his behavior. Repeatedly we could not come up with any specific behavior that Jay was engaging in to account for his so- called lack of popularity. So I designed an experiment.

I suggested, starting tomorrow and lasting for one week until our next session, that Jay greet every single student that he encounters in school with a great big smile and a "Hi, How are you doing?" At this point,

Jay was so desperate that he would have tried anything. He agreed to do the experiment for one week.

At our very next session, Jay came into the room deliriously happy, screaming, "I'm popular. I'm popular. We did it. I'm popular". After listening to Jay's exuberance, and enjoying his happiness rather than the unhappiness that was so previously prevalent, I told Jay that the experiment was not over. We had to find out why it worked. Jay had no ideas why this miracle of his becoming popular over night had occurred. So this time I sent Jay back to school to ask, if he could, some of his new friends just how this shift in their behavior had taken place. Jay agreed.

At our next session, Jay's exuberance was gone, but he was genuinely very happy, contented, and at peace with himself and the world. He related that he had asked this very pretty girl who now was his friend how come she had changed her attitude toward him. He related that she related that all these months in school he looked so angry that she did not dare approach him to talk to him. Now that he was smiling, she felt comfortable to approach him and to talk to him. And all the other kids felt the same way. Jay had been communicating negatively to his classmates. He was depressed and the depression registered as anger so kids avoided him. Once he communicated positively, he received a positive return.

What is important in understanding "The Case of Jay" is that the negative communication was taking place both externally and internally. The real "cure" took place once Jay stopped beating himself up, when he stopped that negative internal communication. Of course, it was the success of the external communication that turned things around, but unless Jay stopped that internal negative communication his depression would not have lifted. Again, the secret ingredient in mental health is communication. Positive communication, especially internally.

CHAPTER 9

Intimacy and Its Secrets

In order to understand the secrets of intimacy, we need to understand that 1) intimacy is the degree of emotional closeness or emotional distance we need in relationships, 2) intimacy is governed by the feelings of Comfortableness (relaxation) or Uncomfortableness (tension) that we experience in relationships, and 3) intimacy is controlled by two basic psychological mechanisms: Fear of Abandonment and Fear of Engulfment. Having made these three statements, let's take a look at how it works.

As children growing up, our major contact with the world is through our parents and families, or their surrogates (people who raise us when we have no parents as well as people whom our own parents delegate that responsibility to). That parental-family interaction teaches us a great deal, things that we are aware of and things that we are not aware of. One of the patterns of behavior that we learned from our families is this degree of closeness or distance we require in a relationship. The degree of emotional distance or closeness in a relationship regulates whether I feel comfortable or uncomfortable in that relationship. Closeness makes some people feel comfortable while other people feel comfortable with distance. Furthermore, some of us feel more comfortable going back and forth between closeness and distance, needing both, while others of us seem to only need one or the other, closeness or distance.

If I grew up in a family where family members communicated openly and honestly with each other, and

I liked that kind of open sharing, most probably in my adult life I would consciously, and even more so unconsciously, want to continue that close kind of intimacy in my adult life. That kind of close, open communication would make me feel relaxed. On the other hand, if I grew up in the kind of family where everyone was rather independent and not so communicative, I most probably would feel more comfortable keeping things to myself, playing it more close to the vest, and I would want that kind of emotional distance in my life. A specific example or two may help to make this point clear.

Several years ago, I saw a couple in their late forties who were in trouble in their marriage. They had been married for 25 years, had four children, and were thinking about divorce. Clearly, it was a tragedy in the making. They just were not getting along. He was very angry with her and was actively seeking a divorce. She was fed up with his complaints and felt that a divorce was much better than living the way they had been living, bickering all the time. As I listened to their complaints about each other, I realized that each of them had a rather different intimacy need. She came from a family where no one communicated openly to each other and she could not understand why all of a sudden he wanted "so much attention." After all, he was "a grown up and not a child." "Children need this kind of attention, not adults" was her way of thinking. He, on the other hand, wanted more closeness from her; or he was going out and getting himself "a girlfriend."

What was happening here is that while the children were growing up, this conflict lay dormant. The husband knew that the wife needed time for the children and he was very happy to allow her this time away from him without his being upset. I say "allow" because in his mind it was his contribution to the family, to deny his own needs for the sake of the family. However, as the children grew up, he began to realize how important it was for him to have this closeness re-established. So he began pushing for it. She on the other hand, once the children were grown up, wanted time for herself. She had sacrificed so much of her own time for the sake of her children. Now that they were on their own, she wanted very much to go back to her need for "space," the pleasure of "being left alone." She thought her husband was "totally unreasonable" for wanting this close intimacy "at your age." He, on the other hand, thought she was "irrational" to let him go "to another woman." In analyzing what had gone on in their childhoods, we found specific reasons as to why she needed space and he needed closeness. He grew up in a close knit, large family where everyone shared and communicated with each other; she grew up in a closed, non-communicative family where everyone went their own way. In raising their own family, their needs for intimacy were sublimated into the needs' of the children. His intimacy needs were governed by the principle of Abandonment, where distance produces tension and anxiety, and her intimacy needs were governed by the Principle of Engulfment, where closeness produces tension and anxiety. Hence, when one partner felt relaxed, the other felt tense. So what do you do with a situation like this?

It was important for both the husband and the wife to learn that neither of them was wrong or "unreasonable." They both had different ways of experiencing and expressing intimacy, a closeness on the part of the husband and a more distant way on the part of the wife. If they were to stay together, we had to understand these differences and see to it that they developed a balance in their existence with each other, sometimes being close and at other times being distant. Furthermore, I explained that as much as we may try we can rarely, if ever, find mates who fit our intimacy needs perfectly. What is important here is to understand that the other person is not deliberately trying to hurt us, but rather is attempting to establish their inner sense of peace and tranquility by attempting to keep the relationship at its optimum closeness or distance level for them.

I also explained to them that there was such a thing as vertical relationships and vertical people as well as horizontal relationships and horizontal people, two concepts that I recently had been working with after having discovered the concepts in analyzing another couple's relationship conflict. Vertical people tend to rely on themselves in functioning daily and go within themselves to think about what they want to do; whereas horizontal people tend to tune into other people, outside of themselves, in making decisions and in their daily functioning. The husband, then, was a Horizontal and the wife was a Vertical. He needed the close intimate contact. She needed a more distant, intimate contact. She loved him as much as he loved her, but she expressed that love differently, in a more distant fashion.

When I explained it to them, the wife turned to me and said with a big smile on her face, "Now I know why he's crazy. He's a damn horizontal." And the husband smiled and said, "And she's a crazy vertical." Because managed care did not allow them to continue beyond a limited number of sessions, I never had the opportunity to complete my work with this couple. Although I did not see them after this, I believe they decided to stay together and work on developing a balance between closeness and distance in their relationship. Verticals and horizontals can live in harmony with each other as long as they understand that their emotional needs are based on a genuine intimacy need that goes way back to childhood which requires patience, hard work, balance, and respect. A more detailed description of this case can be found in the chapter on Making Relationships Work, showing how it was worked out in psychotherapy.

Coming back to the two basic mechanisms that control intimacy, the need for closeness (The Principle of Fear of Abandonment) and the need for distance (The Principle of Fear of Engulfment), it is not difficult to understand these concepts, and what this middle-aged couple went through, if we realize that coming from a background where getting close to people made the husband feel happy as a child, while getting close to people, for the wife, tended to make her feel uncomfortable, about to be criticized, and put down. It all depends on what we went through in our childhoods and how it affected us. We learn emotional closeness or distance in our childhoods, and those patterns of emotional closeness or distance stay with us for the rest of our lives.

The psychological strategy here is very clear. If we want our children to become emotionally close and to enjoy intimacy, then we have to provide them with the opportunity in our families, schools, and religious activities to have positive intimate relationships that they can carry into adulthood. Let me emphasize this: *My Personal Experience Has Been That Unless We Learn It In Childhood, It May Be Nearly Impossible To Learn It In Adulthood.* If you are experiencing difficulty in your own intimate relationship, whether in a marriage or a dating situation, take a look at your own intimacy closeness or distance need as well as that of your partner. Start by communicating to yourself about it, then extend the communication to your mate. See what you both can come up with in finding a balance for yourselves. The communication process involves Recognition, Discussion, Brainstorming, and Resolution.

More about resolution will be found in the next section under the heading of Problem Solving and Conflict Resolution.

CHAPTER 10

Communicating Sexually

Sex is a problem for everyone. We either need too much of it, or we do not need enough of it. We are oversexed and disgusting, or undersexed and frigid. No one seems to have the right balance. Sex is probably the most misunderstood drive that mankind possesses. Sex has brought down governments, disrupted nations from operating, disrupted relationships, and destroyed many marriages. It has created both joy and pain to a rather large percentage of our population. Different people view sex from vastly different points of view. It can be seen as a wonderful way to reduce tension, or an outright sin.

To begin with, sex is an appetite. We all have an appetite for food, but that appetite varies widely among most of us. What we like and do not like in the way of food is pretty clear to us. That some of us have a suppressed appetite, or an overactive appetite, is also known to us. When we eat we are also aware that a reduction in tension occurs. Eating with other people may increase or decrease our appetite. Will knowing all of this help us make sex a less traumatic activity? Not at all.

Sex stands in a category all by itself. While sex gives us a mechanism by which to reduce tension and stress, the opposite takes place. More often than not, sex increases our tension. We tend to feel helpless (inadequate), angry, depressed, guilty, anxious, and ashamed about sex. What could be a mechanism to bring people together tends to pull us apart. In order for sex to work in our everyday life, we need a basic understanding of the sexual differences between men and women, i.e., how sex operates differently in men and women; a respect for those differences; and above all else, an ability to communicate, both internally and externally.

When I am out lecturing to single, separated, and divorced groups, I always ask the women, "What do men want from women?" Invariably, the women respond in unison, "Sex." And when I ask the men what do women want from men, the answer comes up "Communication." Women need to communicate before they have sex, whereas men need to have sex before we open up and communicate. Aside from the fact that little girls learn to talk things out and little boys learn to punch each other in resolving conflicts, there is another basic physiological difference that may account for this sex vs. communication and communication vs. sex difference in men and women.

Because of our basic sexual equipment, men tend to heat up sexually much faster than women. Hence, men may not need to communicate first before becoming ready to engage in sex. Women, on the other hand, tend to have different sexual apparatus and may require a longer, communicative period of time in order to prepare for sex. As Dr. John Gray told his audiences when he appeared on Broadway, men are like microwave ovens, quick to heat up, while women are more like a conventional oven, slower to heat up.

No matter how you define it or describe it, good sex is very much related to good communication on at least two levels. The first level is the internal communication level within a person so that they are aware of what feels good within their own bodies. If I do not know what makes me feel good, how can I know to seek and repeat that pleasure another time? Knowledge from within my body gives me control over my ability to meaningfully seek that sexual pleasure.

The second level of communication takes place in good sex in the form of communication between the partners before, during, and after sex. Good communication during sex allows the partners to enhance their sexual contact and pleasures by telling each other what is pleasing and sexually gratifying. It also allows us to stimulate each other with words, gestures, and visual cues that further increase the pleasure of the activity. If I see you get excited, then I become excited at your excitement! We then mutually turn each other on simply by showing openly our emotional pleasure in the activity, and the sexual pleasure increases.

Some years ago, I developed what I called The Communicating Sexually Checklist. If you answer the questions honestly, and practice them faithfully, your sex life should bring you greater pleasure. Here is the checklist:

THE COMMUNICATINC SEXUALLY CHECK-LIST

1. What do you communicate to your partner during sex? Is s/he responsive? What does your partner communicate to you?

2. Are you aware of your own feelings, thoughts, ideas, and sensations during sexual relations?

3. Are you aware of your partner's feelings, thoughts, ideas, and sensations during sexual relations?

4. Do you communicate what you need sexually? To yourself? To your partner?

5. Do you know what you need sexually?

6. Do you know what your partner needs?

7. Do you ever ask your partner what s/he needs? Can they respond to your inquiry?

8. Do you think about sex? Before? After? During? What do you think about during sex?

9. Have you ever thought about sex in terms of it being a learned activity requiring further education?

10. Are you free enough to talk about sexuality with your partner to the point of being able to take criticism and/or constructive suggestions?

11. Do you ever analyze and evaluate your own sexual behavior?

12. How free are you to try new and perhaps different things sexually?

13. Have you ever wondered what the "sexual gourmets" do that you may not be doing?

14. Do you ever watch X-rated movies?

15. Does specialized language turn you or your partner on? Or off?

16. Does specialized attire increase or decrease your sexual experience? Have you ever tried it?

17. Do sexual fantasies increase your sexual experience? Have you ever tried it?

18. Do you know and can you name any sexual fantasies?

19. Are there any sexual accoutrements available that might increase the sexual experience? For you? For your partner?

20. Do different positions create different sexual results? For you? For your partner?

21. Do erotica, i.e., books, pictures, movies, etc., add anything to the sexual relationship?

22. Do different places, i.e., couch, chair, kitchen table, etc., add anything to the sexual relationship?

23. Does watching self-stimulation of your partner do any thing for the sexual relationship? Good or bad?

24. Does "gourmet touching," i.e., nails, massage, do anything for the sexual relationship?

25. Does "risky sex" do anything for the sexual relationship?

26. Do teasing, playfulness, voyeurism, and/or exhibitionism do anything for the sexual relationship?

27. Can you openly talk about sex to your partner?

28. Can you remember good or great past sexual experiences? And can they be duplicated?

29. Does talking about sex or past sexual experiences turn you on?

30. Have you ever had a course in sexuality?

31. ARE YOU CONCERNED WITH AIDS AND OTHER SEXUALLY TRANSMITTED DISEASES? Do you make it a point to discuss these issues with your partner? How do you communicate it? Are you satisfied with the results?

Work on communicating sexually. It not only could enhance your sex life, it could also take the edge off of your everyday, routine living. Sex is supposed to reduce tension for us. Make it work for you. If sex makes you feel helpless (inadequate), angry, depressed, guilty, anxious, or ashamed, talk it out with your partner. If that does not work, find a therapist that you can talk with and work it through. Too many of us do not have a good sex life because we just do not work on it. It's worth working on.

CHAPTER11

Making Relationships Work

Having successful intimate relationships is one of the most difficult and elusive accomplishments for both men and women. Judging from our horrible national statistics, 50% of first marriages end up in divorce while 66 2/3 of our second marriages end up in divorce. That means that half of all first marriages end up in divorce and two thirds of our second marriages end up in divorce. Besides the negative national statistics, most of us know couples who are grossly unhappy in their marriages but stay together for one reason or another. So knowing how to put a relationship together becomes extremely important for a clear majority of us.

To begin with, in order to put an intimate relationship together we need to understand a great deal about the human psyche and how it works. We also need to have some understanding of the basic mechanisms that govern relationships as well as an understanding of how these mechanisms operate differently in different people. Finally, we have to have an understanding of the basic differences that exist between men and women, and even between women and women, and men and men, culturally and socially.

Strange as it may seem, the human psyche is not particularly geared to helping us make relationships work. Our egos are extremely defensive. We tend not to see our own faults, yet we are experts on the other guy's faults. Hence, we get a one-sided view of the relationship. We get a distorted view of the relationship because we only see one side of it. Even when we are told about the other side, we discount it or do not believe it. Hence, we are at a disadvantage right from the outset because of our own defensiveness.

The first strategy in making a relationship work is to nullify our own defensiveness by listening quite attentively to the other side and trying to imagine ourselves in their position. Once we understand where the other person is coming from we can put that together with our own position; that allows us to assess the entire picture, preventing us from coming to false conclusions. Of course, the backbone in any relationship involves open, honest, good communication.

Several years ago, I began working in co-joint therapy with a middle-aged couple. I call it co-joint therapy rather than marriage counseling because we worked on a much deeper level than what is customarily called marriage counseling. The husband, Jake, was seeking a divorce, but before going ahead with it he wanted to give his wife "another chance." Harriet, his wife, was a simple woman who was tired of hearing Jake's complaints. She was generally content with the marriage; after all, they had been married for 25 years and had managed to raise four children, the youngest, and last of their children living home, was about to go off to college. Jake thought that all their marital problems were caused by Harriet, and Harriet thought that while she might not be "perfect," it was Jake's constant complaining that pulled them apart. Jake felt unloved and rejected. Harriet felt invaded and overrun by Jake's "constant need for attention."

In situations such as these, I usually like to go back to the individual's childhood to understand just what their needs are and how they came to develop these particular needs. Harriet suggested that Jake go first in our joint discussion in as much as he had "so much to complain about."

Jake grew up in a large family where there was a great deal of honesty, openness, communication, and camaraderie. His older sisters were very close and "good" to Jake, often babysitting or just taking care of him. He, in turn, as he grew up, was very loving and giving to his younger siblings, who always appreciated his kindness to them. During his marriage to Harriet, there was never time to sit around and ponder what he was or was not getting out of this marriage. He worked two jobs to put his kids through college and or technical training, while Harriet busied herself, working part-time or taking care of the children and the house. Now that there were fewer pressures on the family, Jake began to reach out to Harriet for a closer relationship. Harriet felt uncomfortable about that. Jake first threatened Harriet by saying he would find someone else if she was not interested in him, then later came up with, "You don't love me...if you loved me, you wouldn't..." and then he would insert various things she did not do with or for him, becoming depressed over the entire relationship with her. As time went on, he became more and more depressed over his lack of an intimacy with Harriet, and at one point his primary care physician wanted to put him on an anti-depressant medication. He was really convinced that Harriet did not love him anymore and speculated aloud that perhaps she had someone else.

When Jake finished telling his story, Harriet quietly looked over to me and slowly began. She was very much in love with Jake. He is a "good and decent man," something very important for Harriet. "Jake needs so much attention. I can't take it...When the children were small we were so busy working together, building a future...Now that I can finally have some peace and quiet, Jake starts to pull at me...It's those damn sisters of his who babied him when he was growing up." As I pointed out earlier, Harriet was an expert on Jake, just as Jake was an expert on Harriet, but Harriet was not focusing on herself. Neither was Jake. So, I interrupted her and asked her to tell me about her own childhood.

Harriet grew up in a slightly smaller family than Jake did, a family that rarely sat down to talk to each other, a family that was dominated by her father's drinking and anger. She recalled how she would run and hide when her father came home for fear that he would go on a violent, angry rampage over something that was not done correctly in the family home that day. Honesty, open communication and comradeship were nowhere to be found in her childhood background. The anger and rage often was fueled by alcohol and her father's excessive drinking. Keeping to yourself was the best way to survive. In her marriage to Jake, she was very contented and happy "just to be left alone," something Jake gave her up until recently when they did not have to worry about money or raising the children. Her question to me was, "Why can't Jake just leave things the way they are?" Now that they both gave their sides to the story and they had answered my inquiry into their childhoods, they both turned to me for some feedback. I began by explaining that relationships, broadly speaking, fall into two categories: Horizontal Relationships and Vertical Relationships. People who are brought up in families where there is an openness, honesty, sharing and communication tend to look to other people in making decisions and in their functioning. They enjoy that horizontal sharing. Other people who are raised in families where the atmosphere is more closed, non-communicative, and less "user-friendly" tend to be more Vertical, they make decisions by going into themselves and tend to look to themselves for ways of handling everyday situations. They have no need to consult others.

After explaining the concept of Vertical and Horizontal functioning in minute detail, I then turned to

Jake and said, "Harriet is a damn Vertical!" at which point Jake broke out in a great grin, leaving no sign of his depression. Jake was overwhelmingly happy that Harriet still loved him, and it was this vertical residue from her childhood that was interfering with their relationship. Jake then said, "Now I know why she is impossible. She is a Vertical." At that moment, Harriet broke out in a grin and said: "Now I know why Jake is so crazy. He's a Damn Horizontal." What took place at that moment was a major relief for both of them. They were given a concept to explain why they had not been getting along, a concept that did not blame either one of them, a concept that could help them reduce their defensiveness while learning about the human psyche, their own human psyches in particular. While this couple was far from successfully completing their therapeutic goal of resolving their differences, they were put on the right track of understanding each other and coming to understand each other's genuine needs, needs which have their roots deeply embedded in their early childhoods. What followed in their treatment was a working through of these differences whereby they learned to respect each other's needs and they had to learn how to accommodate their mate's needs when the situation called for it.

The concept of balance comes into play at this point. There has to be a balance with regard to whose needs get satisfied at any given moment. As much as possible, we should balance out whose needs get satisfied, although there can be exceptions to the balance rule when one of the mates finds that their need at a particular juncture is a ten, on a scale from one to ten, and the other mate has a conflicting need of much less intensity, say a five or six. However, such exceptions to the rule should not be an ordinary, every time occurrence. If exceptions become too prominent, then direct communication needs to be instituted to resolve the conflict.

I would like to add a word about the concept of Horizontal and Vertical Relationships because you will undoubtedly not find them so readily in the psychology literature. I discovered the concept while working with a young couple several years earlier. There, too, the husband loved his wife very much but generally did not seek her out in making decisions and in regard to his many activities. In that case, the husband was the vertical and the wife was the horizontal. Vertical and horizontal do not depend upon gender. Their existence depends upon early childhood training. The lesson to be gained here is that when people reject us it is important to find out where THEY are coming from. It may not always be us as we so often assume. Rejection usually takes place in relationships and it behooves us to become a little more assertive in delving into what it is that we, ourselves, might have done to create the rejection. More often than not, the problem may be easily fixed. It is the defensiveness that prevents us from looking closely and then applying conflict resolution techniques, which are discussed in the next section, to help us make the relationship work. By nullifying our defensiveness we can take a giant step toward understanding things and then making relationships work.

CHAPTER 12

When Communicating With Others Fail

If communication is the secret ingredient in mental health, and communicating keeps us mentally healthy, what do we do when communication with others fails? Undoubtedly, breakdowns in communication will occur, and we should expect them to occur, so we should be prepared to deal with the situation.

Communication tends to do two things for us. First, it allows us to get our feelings and viewpoints aired, and secondly, it allows us the opportunity to change things in our environment when people listen and respond Positively to our communications. Both of these activities create a reduction in tension through communication. When communication with others fails, we lose the opportunity to effect those environmental changes we had hoped to achieve. Hence, tension may increase. Communication tends to decrease tension and a breakdown in communication tends to increase tension. In as much as it is in our best interest to decrease tension, it becomes extremely important to find a way to communicate what is inside of us even in situations where our chance of reaching the other person is gravely diminished. Even if there is virtually no hope of effecting a change in the situation, in order to stay mentally healthy it becomes imperative that we find some way of getting our feelings, thoughts, and needs on the table. Of course, there are exceptions to this rule, and psychology is full of exceptions to the rule; nevertheless, unless we are able to get it out of our systems, we will be subject to developing psychological symptoms such as anxiety, depression, and even physical pain due to this blockage. Chapter 6, on How Symptoms Are Developed, outlines the procedure in detail.

How many times have we heard ourselves, or someone in our families say, "I don't want to talk about it," or "What good is talking about it going to do?" or "I just won't talk to him or her anymore!" or "We haven't talked to each other for years, so why start now?" All of these approaches to life end up hurting us. It is extremely important not to allow anything to interfere with our communicating, especially within one's own family. PERSONALLY, I HAVE MADE IT A RULE IN MY OWN LIFE TO STAY WITH HONEST, OPEN COMMUNICATION AS MUCH OF THE TIME AS IS HUMANLY POSSIBLE (WITHOUT BECOMING SELF-DESTRUCTIVE).

Honesty is an important component here. Unless I am honest with myself, then all else that follows will be distorted and false. Unless I am honest with other people, then all else that follows will be distorted and false, and reality will be lost. Hence, honesty is my first resource when communication breaks down. I begin by expressing my feelings and thoughts about the breakdown in communication. It might come out something like, "I feel upset that we cannot talk to each other... If we are ever going to understand each other and work things out, we must find a way to listen to each other and really try to be patient with each other... I feel very sad about it... And I have been thinking about our not getting along and I really want it to be resolved... What can I do to make things work?"

If my attempt at breaking through the roadblock fails, I then shift my communication, gearing toward resolving the breakdown in communication to an expression of my own viewpoint of the situation itself: "In as much as I cannot get you to reconsider your position and viewpoint and talk further with me, I would appreciate if you would listen to some of my thought and feelings... By understanding where I am coming from, it may help you grasp the situation a little differently... Could you at least hear me out without committing yourself to anything except listening?"

When a breakdown in communication occurs, a rather unique and important opportunity presents itself. Handled properly, it could lead us to breakthrough and gain new insight and develop a closer relationship with the other person. Handled incorrectly, it could lead us into depression and despair. Many years ago, a close friend of mine became stubbornly angry with me. Although I tried talking to him, he closed off and would only say, "There is nothing to talk about," followed by his avoidance of me. I spoke to his wife, asking her for some direction in resolving the problem, but she had no idea what this was all about or what to do about it. After ten days of distance and avoidance, I decided to go over to his house and confront the issue head on. Armed with only my own inner feelings and thoughts, and not knowing why he was specifically angry with me (he either did not know fully or just refused to say), I communicated the following to him, "I do not know why you are so angry with me... What I do know is that I feel terrible that I did something that upset you... We have been friends for a long time and I would never knowingly do anything to hurt you... I cannot tell you how upset I am that I must have done something so hurtful that caused you to be so angry with me... I want you to know that I apologize to you for upsetting you so much. I'm really sorry." What I did in this situation, where communication from my friend was not forthcoming, was to reach inside of myself and express those thoughts and feelings as they existed in me. I also apologized for "upsetting" him rather than apologizing for doing something wrong in as much as I really felt that I did nothing wrong, but felt genuinely sorry he was upset. I also did not address the frustration I felt in his refusing to communicate. Choosing not to talk about that frustration, I reasoned, was a good choice. Talking about what he did or did not do would be destructive because it would have in all probability led nowhere except to further conflict. At any rate, the friendship was preserved. He accepted my apology and we have been friends ever since. I never found out just why he was so angry with me, but several months later he and his wife separated and ultimately divorced. I always felt that his being angry with me was really related to what was going on in his marriage and he just took it out on me. The chapter on defense mechanisms calls this displacement, when we are angry with one person and take it out on another person. We often do that to each other without realizing that it is happening.

By reaching in and communicating what was inside of me preserved the relationship and our friendship. There are other times, however, when the goal in a situation where communication with others fail is not to re-cement the relationship, but merely to get your own feelings and thoughts expressed so you are not left with those headaches, or stomach upsets. In such a situation, I might say something like, "I know you do not want to hear it, but I have a need to say it... I think that you are absolutely wrong for being angry with me... I saw the situation totally different than you did... I never intended to hurt you... I would go out of my way not to hurt you... I feel you are unfair to me and if you think it is worth breaking up a friendship over this issue, go right ahead...I do not think so and I would never do this to you."

In each of the situations just cited, the communication continued. I cannot stress enough the importance of not cutting communication off EXCEPT IN RARE, EXCEPTIONAL INSTANCES. Even when others do not respond to us, it is extremely important to find a way to communicate what is inside of us. In so doing, not only do we "get it out of our system," we also do something that is ego strengthening. We took care of our need to be mentally and physically healthy. We got our point expressed. Whether it was well accepted by others or not – we have no control over that. We can only control ourselves. And that is exactly what we did. We did the best possible thing we could do under the circumstances. We did everything in our power to make our viewpoint clear. That takes a great deal of time, energy and aplomb, all of which should make us feel proud of ourselves. Being proud of ourselves in a losing situation is nothing to sneeze at! That's what I mean when I say it is ego strengthening, being proud of ourselves even under the most adverse conditions, when we are not sure that others will really respond to what we have to say. If nothing else, keep communicating for yourself. Unless you are really overdoing it, open, honest communication is the way to go. Even when communication with others fails.

CHAPTER 13

Secrecy, Silent Anger, and Loneliness

Secrecy, silent anger and loneliness seem to go together. There are many people who are prone to just keeping things to themselves, not revealing themselves to other people for a variety of reasons ranging from not wanting others to have information that potentially could hurt them to just preferring not to have their business known by others. What these people do not realize is that they are engaging in repressive behavior that utilizes the psychological mechanism of Repression. In essence, repression involves "just putting things out of your mind." Unfortunately, when we just put things out of our mind, like all matter, it has to go somewhere. Where it usually goes is into some symptom such as headaches, stomachaches, and the like. Freud called use of the mechanism of repression "the royal road to mental illness," meaning that repressed material tends to feed many of the psychological symptoms that mankind tends to experience. So when we engage in keeping things to ourselves, we are really flirting with repression and quite possibly courting disaster. All those times we did not feel physically well, could quite possibly have been related to the fact that we had a lot going on in our heads that just never got expressed externally but did get expressed internally, through physical symptoms. For instance, Dr. Herbert Benson at the Harvard Medical School's Mind-Body Medical Institute tells us that over 60% of all doctor visits are due to psychological reasons rather than for medical reasons. Therefore, while secrecy makes us feel safe from being hurt by other people, it makes us unsafe from being hurt by ourselves. While we are just beginning to uncover the relationship between the mind and the body, it is well known that psychological factors such as repression play an enormous role in weakening our immune system. And we all know what happens when our immune system becomes weakened, physical illness develops. In fact, the term PSYCHONEUROIMMUNOLOGY is a new field of study that has come out of the new understanding of how the mind and body work together.

The specific relationship between anger and hostility, and coronary heart disease is a good example of how the mind affects the body. We now know that anger and hostility causes the platelets in the blood to thicken and become sticky. The sticky platelets then zap onto the fatty deposits in the arteries causing plaque, which in turn results in coronary heart disease. Silent anger, the feelings of anger that are not expressed but kept inside of so many of us, can play a major role in our developing coronary heart disease and many other physical ailments. Hence, it is best not to develop feelings of anger or hostility. But if you do, it is crucial that you talk about it and resolve the underlying conflict. Suppressing or repressing feelings of anger, something that is not that uncommon in present day society, sets us up for serious consequences both mentally and physically. It certainly can lead us into anxiety, depression and personal maladaptive behavior as well as into an exacerbation of any physical symptoms that we may be experiencing. Walking around with silent anger is like walking around with a time bomb inside of yourself. We just do not when it will go off. If you are walking around with this silent anger within you, talk it out. Communication is not only the secret ingredient in mental health, it is your ally in getting rid of that silent anger.

Loneliness is a terrible thing to experience. Yet if we persist in secrecy and silent anger, then loneliness will follow just as night follows day. The more we keep things hidden, the more we will feel lonely and alone. Opening ourselves up to others is a major step toward overcoming loneliness. Dr. Dean Ornish, the well-known cardiologist, in his book on *Reversing Coronary Heart Disease*, points to how important it is for cardiac patients to open themselves up for both psychological and physical reasons, benefiting both the mind and the body. Loneliness is a terrible price to pay for being closed off, in secrecy and in silent anger. So, once again we come back to how very, very important it is for each one of us to work on our own communication skills and to be aware of how important it is to teach these skills to our young.

CHAPTER 14

Hurting and Being Hurt

Hurting and being hurt is an inevitable consequence of everyday living. In fact, it is virtually impossible to be in any relationship that does not result in either our being hurt or in our hurting someone else's feelings. The hurting can be conscious and deliberate, or it can be unconscious and accidental. In either case, the hurting takes place and creates psychic pain for us. In as much as we know and go through such painful experiences, is it not astounding that most of us do not have a strategy for handling hurtful situations. We were never taught anything about expecting them to occur, and certainly we were never given any strategies for handling hurtful situations. We may have been told to "ignore it," or "give it back to them," or "don't take it anymore," but no one told us that it is a natural consequence of all relationships and that we ought to think about developing techniques for handling such situations.

While we may be keenly aware of how other people hurt us, because of the defensiveness of our egos, we rarely are able to see how we hurt other people. In doing marriage and relationship counseling for the past 40 years, I have always found that both husbands and wives typically are keenly astute in seeing how their partners contribute negatively to their relationships, but they are keenly unaware of how they themselves contribute negatively to the disharmony in the relationship. So, one of the first steps in resolving hurtful feelings in a relationship is to see how we ourselves may have contributed to the problem.

Many years ago, I was seeing a man in counseling who was going through what turned out to be a long and protracted divorce. During the many hours that he spent discussing his divorce, he invariably commented bitterly that none of his wife's relatives, toward whom he had been generous and friendly, had bothered to contact him to see "if I am alive or dead." One day he ran into one of these lost in-law relatives. He brought the subject up. He complained to her that while he had called her when she was hospitalized, she had not called him to see how he was doing during the divorce. She replied in surprise, "But don't you remember... You said that you were feeling down and that you wanted to be left alone... That talking about the separation just seemed to make you feel worse... So we left you alone... We didn't want to remind you of Marjorie or the situation." My patient created the situation that made him feel hurt.

By communicating to people we feel have hurt us, we can come to understand and clarify the situation to the point of not hurting any more. By communicating to people who feel that we have hurt them, instead of running away from them, we can come to understand and clarify the situation to the point of not hurting any more.

More years ago that I care to remember, a friend became annoyed at me because I went to a meeting without him. He specifically made a point of telling me that I had hurt his feelings by going to the meeting without him. Whenever that kind of confronting communication takes place, I know something good will come out of it. So I began, "Yes, that's true... I went to the meeting without you... Do you have any idea why I did that, besides the fact it was very selfish of me to go without you... Can you think of any other idea as to why I would go without you? Let me tell you... I did you a great favor by not taking you to the meeting... I knew it was going to be boring and a waste of time... I had to be there so I went... I saved you and did you a great turn by not taking you... You should appreciate it and thank me instead of being annoyed with me." My friend said very little, but it was evident that once I communicated my rationale to him the issue was resolved.

Had I been selfish and guilty of going off without my friend, I would have been honest with him. If I wanted the relationship to continue, I would have apologized to him and given him some reassurance that my selfish behavior would be curtailed. I also would have offered to be open and honest in future dealings prior to the event and not after. If my selfish behavior were to continue, I would expect him not to put up with it and abandon the relationship. Here again, if he were to abandon the relationship, it would be wise of me to look to myself for the breakup of the relationship.

Most of the time we end up hurting each other without realizing it. Hence, it becomes extremely important to communicate how, where, and why we feel hurt without attacking the other person. Attacks only make us defensive to the point of having to deny our part in the negative situation. Merely presenting the facts as we see them while expressing what we feel and think is a far superior approach. Not communicating is the least desirable position to take unless not communicating is a temporary tactic to take prior to opening up full communication. It is full communication, especially as described in the next section, which leads to effective resolution of conflicts. Hurting and being hurt is an inevitable consequence of conflict. Resolving conflicts resolves the hurt.

Part III

Problem Solving
and Conflict Resolution

Success in life cannot take place unless we have some strategies to handle Problem Solving And Conflict Resolution. Rarely does life unfold in a perfect manner. Having strategies to handle the ups and downs of life puts us ahead of the game and gives us The Psychological Edge.

CHAPTER 15

A Model For Conflict Resolution

For the past several years, I have been involved in a program that teaches middle school children how to do problem solving and conflict resolution. It is interesting to observe how 5th, 6th, 7th, and 8th grade boys and girls handle conflict. The boys invariably solve their problems by punching each other out. The girls, on the other hand, are more apt to talk it out, sometimes behind each other's backs. In relationship counseling, the same holds true. The women tend to communicate much more openly than the men, and generally, the men have very poor communication skills when compared to the women. When I am out lecturing to single, separated and divorced groups, I ask the men and women what they want from each other. Invariably the women reply that they want communication from men. Hence, it seems that those patterns set in early childhood continue well into our adult lives and that a model for conflict resolution is something we all need. I wonder how many school shootings and tragedies could have been averted, let alone how many marriages could have been saved, if we were all taught effective problem-solving techniques and conflict resolution procedures when we were kids.

The very first step in any problem-solving, conflict resolution activity is HONESTY. Unless we are honest with ourselves and honest with the other person, any attempt at resolving differences becomes exceedingly difficult. That means that each of the participants must be ready to SAY HONESTLY WHAT THEY FEEL AND THINK and to be able to LISTEN OPENLY AND HONESTLY TO THE OTHER

PERSON, without being defensive or attacking. At any rate, this is how it looks spelled out:

Step 1: Arrange a mutually agreeable time and place to sit down and talk about the problem. Allow no interruptions.

Step 2: Decide who will present their side of the problem first. Express your feelings and thoughts and perceptions. Allow the other person to express their feelings, thoughts and perceptions. Do not attack each other and do not become defensive. Listen attentively to their position. The goal is to understand the other person's position and not to win the argument. Show respect for each other's position and proceed with dignity.

Step 3: Suggest Possible Solutions

Step 4: Try One of the Solutions

Step 5: If The Solution Works, Keep It. If Not, Return To Step 3 and Step 4.

Step 6: Let Go Of Any Residual Negative Thoughts Or Feelings.

In my presentation to the children, I use an illustration from my childhood. When I was growing up, I had two childhood friends, Jay and Bobby. One day Jay and Bobby went to the movies without me. Movies were especially important activities in those pre-television days. Saturday was a day for the movies. Jay and Bobby went to the movies without me. What did I feel? What did I think? I felt hurt and angry. I thought that they were mean to me and that they did not like me anymore and that they did not want to be friends with me anymore. So what did I do? I called Jay and Bobby and I asked to meet with them. We set up a time and place to meet. Bobby was sick, so Jay and I met. We agreed to let me start since I asked for the meeting. "Jay, you and Bobby went to the movies without me." Jay responded, "Yes we did." Jay was a very bright guy and responded to me with his legal, professional voice and stance. So I continued, "Why did you do that?... Didn't you care that you left me out?... I feel hurt and left out... I thought we had a friendship... Don't you want to be friends anymore?... How can you do this to me?... Don't you care?"

Jay cut to the heart of the situation, "Yes we are friends... And yes we care... And we did not intend to hurt you... We feel terrible that you feel so hurt." "Then how could you do this to me?" Jay went on, "It wasn't us.... It was Bobby's father... You know how hot under the collar he gets... If things are not done exactly the way he wants them done he gets outrageous... That's what happened... Bobby's father said that he would drive us to the movies... We tried to call you but your phone was busy... Once we tried you a couple of times Bobby's father got angry and told us to get our coats on, we were going, no more phone calls...And he was not waiting to find out if you could go." I responded, "My mother must have been on the phone with her girlfriend yakking it up... And I know Bobby's father's temper... I feel better knowing that you didn't do it on purpose... And I am glad that we are still friends, but what do we do now?" I felt comfortable asking Jay because Jay was gifted. I once saw his school grades record sheet on the secretary's desk and his lowest grade was a 92, and all the rest were 98's, 96's or 95's. I knew he would come up with something we could try. He did. Jay's idea was to arrange on the Friday, in school, the day before we were to go to the movies, what our plan would be. Hence, we would not have to call each other at the last minute. Great idea (Step 3). We tried it (Step 4). It did not work. The next Friday, Bobby was sick again and we could not follow the plan. Back to the drawing board we went (to

Step 3 again). This time we added the idea that if one of us was not in school on that Friday, planning day, we would call each other up as soon as we got home and finalize our plans. We tried it. This time it worked.

That's the model I have been using with middle school kids. It also happens to be very similar to the kind of problem-solving, conflict resolution that takes place in psychotherapy. If middle school kids understand it and can use it, then it would seem that it would be a snap for adults to use. Unfortunately, step 6 may be one reason that might make the whole procedure fall apart. We really have to let go of the situation once we have worked on it even if we do not get our own way. Resolution means being willing to be flexible enough to accept a solution even if it is less than perfect and not quite what we want. Taking less now may mean more later on. Besides, there is a great deal of wear and tear on the body when conflicts are not resolved. More about letting go in a later chapter, but for now think of the release your body will feel once the conflict is released from your inner psyche.

CHAPTER 16

Resolving Stress and Frustration

There are times in everyday living that are so overwhelming that no amount of reasoning or communication can possibly relieve the pressure that we feel. Such a time occurred in my life when my brother was dying of leukemia. There was very little I could do except to pray and 1 did. It is during such times of stress that having several special techniques to help us reduce tension can be especially appreciated. The techniques for reducing stress and tension which follow not only come in handy in extremely difficult times; they also can be used effectively in handling the tensions and stresses that occur in everyday living.

The first technique 1 rely upon is called the Relaxation Response, developed, scientifically studied and actively recommended by Dr. Herbert Benson at the Harvard Medical School's Mind-Body Medical Institute. Dr. Benson, a cardiologist, was looking for a way to reduce hypertension, high blood pressure. Several groups came to him, telling him how meditation had helped them reduce their everyday stress levels, including their hypertension. He embarked upon a scientific study of the process and came up with what he calls the Relaxation Response. Although this all occurred over 20 years ago, even today the Relaxation Response is taught at the Harvard Medical School and at all the Harvard affiliated hospitals. This is how it works:

1. Find a quiet place where you will not be disturbed, nor interrupted by phone calls.

2. Begin with your feet and ankles. Tighten and then loosen the muscles of your feet and ankles. Next, tighten and loosen or relax the muscles of you calves. Then move up your body to you knees, thighs, stomach and pelvis, chest, back, arms, back of your neck, area around your eyes, and finally your forehead, tightening and then relaxing each group of muscle. This is a preliminary procedure called progressive relaxation.

3. Close your eyes. Begin to take several slow deep breaths

4. On each exhale say the number "one"

5. Keep repeating the number "one" on each exhale for anywhere from 5 to 10 minutes. Allow yourself to feel the tension leaving your body, going down your body and out your toes.

6. If the number "one" is unappealing to you, you can use any simple word or words like " peace," "relax," "tranquility," or any religious word or phrase you choose. The idea is to stay focused on our word and not to keep thinking about what is going on in our daily lives. My own suggestion is to start out with the number "one" until you get your feet wet and then change and make it into something special for yourself.

While the best way to reduce tension, in my opinion, is through communication, we cannot always count on the fact that others will be willing to sit down and communicate with us, and there may be times when we cannot spare the time to sit down and communicate with them, but we always can manage a few minutes to work on our breathing.

Incidentally, there is something also called a mini-relaxation response when you do not have the time to sit quietly and do the regular relaxation response.

Simply keep your eyes open, breath in and out a few times and say "one" or your chosen word as you exhale. You can do this mini-breathing exercise for several breaths. One day while shopping for a new suit, I lost my prescription sunglasses. I was about to have lunch when I discovered they were missing. I was so upset that I could not eat my lunch. My palms were sweaty; my heart was beating a mile a minute and I could feel my whole insides wanting to jump out of my body. I told myself to calm down and relax. But as you all know, that just does not work. So I began to do a mini-relaxation response right at the restaurant. I took 8 breaths, counting "one" on the first exhale, "two" on the second exhale, "three" on the third and "four" on the fourth exhale. I then counted "four" on the fifth exhale, "three" on the sixth, "two" on the seventh exhale and finally "one" on the eighth exhale. With those 8 breaths I became calm, my insides relaxed, and I was able to eat and enjoy my lunch. IT WORKS! TRY IT!

Another tension reducing technique that I use is called Visual Imagery. Again, I can use it alone. I do not need anyone to help me reduce my tension except myself. This is how it works:

1. Close your eyes and simply bring to mind or remember a scene or activity that was peaceful or relaxing. Something like being at the beach or mountains. Either re-live that experience or conjure up a new scene that will be relaxing. Some people take themselves to the shore; others re-live a pleasurable vacation they had been on. Recently, I saw a woman who was in a great deal of discomfort due to a tough bout with radiation therapy. When I suggested that she close her eyes and conjure up some memories of a recent trip she had taken, she thought I was "crazy." But before long she was far away from her pain, telling me about all

the wonderful sights she was visualizing right before her eyes. It can work for you too.

While working with another patient just down the hall in the hospital who was in pain in the thigh section of both legs, he told me that "cold" makes his pain diminish. I suggested that he visualize himself sitting in a cold stream with the cold water washing over his burning thighs. He did it and it helped. He did me one better. He visualized the cold water of a Maine ocean scene from his memories of his last Maine vacation that he assured me would be colder than my stream.

2. You can make up any visualization that you like. Some of mine include visualizing: a waterfall, water cascading down a mountain, swan floating across a mirrored lake, plane coming in for a landing at night (especially over New York City), looking up at the stars at night while lying on a blanket (courtesy of a patient), lying on a blanket at the beach, and smelling the salt water air and watching all the people on the beach against a blue sky while hearing the waves break on the shore.

Both the Relaxation Response and the use of Visual Imagery require work and practice. Their full relaxative effect may not be immediate, but they sure can bring you periods of relaxation once you have developed the necessary skills required to bring out their full effect. Paramount in working with these two techniques is the fact that most of us will find some excuse to avoid doing them. Either we just cannot find the right time to do them, or they just do not do anything for me, or I just cannot concentrate, or we just forget to do them. In a sense, it is much like the resistances we all put up that prevent us from dieting and losing weight. Take the time and make the effort. Read more about these techniques and develop their gift to you. Where else can you find the keys to relaxation and tranquility without paying a heavy price for it? Use your own mind to help your body heal itself. The personal gains can be enormous.

CHAPTER 17

Letting Go

Perhaps one of the greatest assets we can have in helping us with everyday living, in problem solving and conflict resolution, is the ability to let go. Letting go of a problem or conflict is not as easy as it sounds. As so many of my patients tell me when I push them to let go: "It's easier said than done." Not only is it a difficult thing to do, it is also a very tricky thing to do. If we let go of a problem too soon, there could be major psychological and even physical repercussions. Likewise, if we hang onto a problem too long, there could be major psychological and physical repercussions. Hence, timing and a thorough understanding of the issues are paramount in being able to achieve an effective, healthy letting go. Letting go can be either healthy or unhealthy depending on the timing and understanding of the problem or conflict. Let's see if I can give you an example that clarifies this point.

If I am hurt and angry with a friend of mine because he went off to an activity without either telling me or inviting me to that activity, and another mutual friend tells me to "forget about it," this is how it plays out. If on the surface I just let it go while inside of me I am hurting and boiling over with anger, I am apt to develop such psychological and physical symptoms as headaches, stomach upsets, tensions, an inability to sleep through the night, and sudden outbursts of anger or depression, just to name a few of the things that could happen to me. Some people even break out in hives. A healthy letting go means that my outer behavior and inner feelings are in harmony, in agreement. Being calm and forgiving on the outside while being hurt and angry on the inside sets me up for the development of some serious symptoms.

On the other hand, if my friend apologizes to me and I still do not let go because he just keeps doing things like that and I cannot forgive him, I leave myself open to developing such symptoms as headaches, stomach upsets, tensions, an inability to sleep through the night, and sudden outbursts of anger or depression. These are the exact same symptoms that I might have developed had I immediately forgotten about it without having resolved my inner feelings and frustrations. So how do we let go in a healthy way?

Letting go in a healthy way means first, thinking about it by asking ourselves a few important questions. How hurt and angry am I? On a scale of 1 to 10, where would I place my feelings? If it means a great deal to me, say 6 or above, I would not immediately let it go. I would think about it further. If it means very little to me, 5 or below, I would let it go without worrying about having a residual build up of feelings that might back-up to create problems for me. When my feelings are minimally upset, I can let go at that point if I choose to do so without fearing symptom repercussions.

If, on the other hand, the situation really bothered me, with ratings in the upper half of the scale, I would have to think about the situation much more, looking at it from many different angles, like looking at the different facets of a diamond. I need to understand the situation much more in order to come up with something that would allow me to let go. I do not want to let go and have that situation come back and haunt me by my developing symptoms after I thought I resolved it. So I might ask myself something like: Did I play a part in contributing to the problem? To what extent did I make this negative situation happen? What are my alternatives to resolving the problem? Will communication work? What can I communicate that might make it work through? Can I ask for help from others? Will sharing our feelings and perception of the situation do anything?

If I had made every effort to resolve the situation and all my efforts failed, I would have to let go of the situation. Letting go under these circumstances means not allowing myself the opportunity to continue to think about the situation. I must realize that I decided to let it go, to move on to other things. In order to accomplish my goal of letting go I must be consciously aware of where my mind chooses to focus. Our minds tend to focus quite automatically, what Freud called unconsciously. In order to really let go I may have to do what I call "manually override" the situation. Not to allow myself to go back to it automatically. So when I begin again to think about the situation or start to talk about it, I quickly must catch myself and shift my focus from thinking about the situation to thinking about something else, anything other than the situation I want to get away from. If I begin to talk about it, even to add something new, I must stop myself. The key here is to do manually what was taking place automatically by monitoring it and exerting my conscious control over it. I decided that I was going to let go because that was the best and healthiest position I could take. If I fall back on my decision, then I have the responsibility and power to control it by focusing on other discussions and other thoughts. It takes a bit of work and energy to monitor the situation, but each one of us has the ability and power within us to accomplish it.

In resolving the situation, if I had to concede a point or two, I must remember that I have to let go of that concession as well. Is it such a terrible thing to do to admit that we contributed to the situation even though the other person will not admit their part? Tit for tat never did anyone any good.

If the other person wins an argument with me, I have the power to let it go or dispute it all over again. By my deciding that I will let it go does not necessarily mean that I am weak. It means that I have made a decision that allows things to be resolved. As long as there is no residual build-up of negative feelings, the decision can be viewed as a good and healthy one.

Letting go also means letting go of the negative feelings about ourselves. None of us are so perfect that we can go through life without making innumerable mistakes and errors. Presidents, Kings, and mortal men and women make mistakes. To dwell on our mistakes is human but not healthy. The next chapter in particular deals with this issue of our negative self-communications. Letting go means letting go of our own grudges, angers, hatreds, resentments, injustice collections, and our own self-criticism.

The real meaning of letting go lies ultimately with our ability to practice and engage in forgiveness. To be able to forgive others and ourselves for whatever wrongdoing occurred, in actuality or in our perceptions of what actually occurred. We need to practice forgiveness. Of others and ourselves. If you have any doubts about it, read Mitch Albom's book, *Tuesdays With Morrie*. As Morrie lay immobile with ALS, Lou Gehrig's Disease, waiting to meet his Maker, he desperately wanted us to know that practicing forgiveness is one major lesson that we all should learn before we leave this earth.

Forgiveness is the real key to letting go. Learning to forgive others and ourselves for our shortcomings and mistakes in life is undoubtedly one of the most important, powerful lessons of life. Those who have learned forgiveness have been blessed with a gift, the key to opening the door of calmness and tranquility. Forgiveness is one of the major cornerstones in life that allows us peace and tranquility in everyday living.

CHAPTER 18

Spirituality, Humor, and Cognitive Reconstruction

What do Spirituality, Humor, and Cognitive Restructuring have in common? They are three roads that we can take to give us CONTROL over our own well-being. Incidentally, they also are three important elements of the Mind-Body Medicine Program at the Harvard Medical School's Mind-Body Medical Institute which is devoted to helping people develop effective approaches to their own health and well being.

The key word in the last paragraph is CONTROL. When we can control ourselves and our environment (the world around us) we develop that sense of relaxation, calmness, and inner peace that reduces tension and anxiety. It also does a great deal in preventing us from feeling depressed in our everyday living. Control makes us feel less pressured. It allows us a foot hole in our problem solving and conflict resolution endeavors as we go through our daily activities.

Spirituality

Spirituality has become more prominent in American life in the late 90's, especially in the field of healing and wellness. Mainstream medicine has begun to take a closer look. Many hospitals are beginning to establish what they call Complimentary Medicine divisions that include spirituality as a healing tool. Columbia University's Presbyterian Medical Center in

New York City has been conducting research in this field under the expert direction of Dr. Nemet Oz, the cardiac surgeon who gave Frank Torre, Joe Torre of New York Yankee fame's brother, his transplanted heart. Research has already taught us that praying for patients helps those patients recover more quickly after surgery than those patients who received no prayer. In fact, it has been reported in one study that the patients who did not know whether they were being prayed for recovered from their illness faster than those that did not receive prayer. So all in all, there seems to be something here that may benefit us all. As was said earlier, perhaps spirituality has its greatest meaning for us humans because psychologically it gives us something very specific we can do to help ourselves, especially in the area of control. Prayer is something we can do that allows us to cut into that empty, helpless, depressing feeling when things in our lives are out of control. Like when a serious illness strikes our families or us.

In spite of its importance, spirituality is difficult to define. At least, I have a difficult time defining it. So I asked a close friend of mine whom I believe is spiritual to define it for me. This is how he put it, "Spirituality is a feeling of oneness with the Universe... It is different than religion... Having spirituality means that you are in harmony with the world... All is well... And you are at peace within yourself and the world... Consequently, very little is troubling to you." I not only like the definition, I like the relaxed, calm state that results from being spiritual.

Spirituality is something worth pursuing. My advice to you is the same as I give to my patients. Talk about it, think about it, and read about it. It is another way to find peace and harmony in our daily living. Certainly that is what we all are after.

Humor

Humor and laughter make life more bearable. It is another piece of life we all could use more of. Unfortunately, most of us either forget to use humor in our daily functioning, or we complain that there is not too much to laugh and joke about amidst all of our problems. In a sense, we need to learn how to use humor to lighten our burden in everyday living because no one ever taught us how to use it to benefit us. Finding something to laugh about in the middle of a difficult situation can be a great tension reducer. So can the ability to laugh at ourselves help reduce tension. I can recall over and over again in disagreements with friends and relatives throughout my own lifetime, when I finally was able to see the other person's point of view, admit that I was wrong, and to be able to laugh at my own obtuseness. Invariably I would experience a great sense of relief followed by a very discernible reduction in tension. I have used humor quite often in difficult moments in doing psychotherapy for many years to reduce tension.

Several years ago, a new patient joined my Symptom Reduction Group in Pain Management. In response to my suggestion that she tell the group about some of the problems she was going through, she began detailing some of the problems she had encountered in her lifetime which led up to her joining the group. As a teenager, she had a colostomy and has been wearing a bag for over 30 years; she has Crohn's disease, which leaves her in a great deal of pain due to the ulceration of her digestive system; and recently she was diagnosed with cancer. At that point, the entire group, including my new patient, all became so depressed that we felt like jumping off of the nearest tall building. Instead, I turned to her and said, "Helen, what on earth are you doing here? You should be dead ten times over." Helen broke out laughing so loud that I thought that she would fall off her chair. So did the group. When it quieted down, I explained to Helen and the group just what I meant. The bad news was that Helen had many serious medical problems, but the good news was that Helen had managed to survive them all, a magnanimous accomplishment in its own right, that Helen herself failed to recognize and underscore what was a rather positive achievement in her lifetime. She was winning the battle against all these serious illnesses, yet she failed to take credit for it. That is something we will address in a moment. For the present, it is important to recognize how the devastatingly seriousness of the moment was broken with the humor and that the group could go on to look at some other rather important issues, how Helen was constantly underrating herself.

Humor is important in our daily lives. Research is coming to show us that all sorts of good physiological changes take place when humor is present. Use it, look for it, and find it. Make it part of your life.

Cognitive Reconstruction

People communicate on two separate planes. One plane is between people, like between you and me. The other plane is within oneself, like between me and me. When I personally do something well, I may compliment myself. When I do not do something well, I do not compliment myself, but I might criticize myself. That's how most of us operate. We communicate with others and ourselves. Some of us are aware of our own internal communications, what we say to ourselves, while some of us are unconscious of them, and are unaware that there is a whole network of communications going on inside of us. These internal communications reflect how and what we think about our own functioning and ourselves.

Cognitive Reconstruction focuses on that internal communication between me and me. A good example is Helen, the pain patient. She is so very much like most of us. We take credit for messing things up in our lives, but we rarely take credit for the good things we do. When we mess things up, the goal should be thinking of ways to correct the error rather than thinking how dumb of us that we messed it up. How we think about these situations and ourselves has an enormous impact on our behavior, feelings, and self-esteem. When I am on my way to give a lecture, if I begin to think negatively about the lecture, like the audience will not be receptive tonight, or they just will not like what I am going to say, or they are just going to be a mean group tonight, I will get myself depressed before I get there. And I will not feel like giving the lecture. However, if on the way to the lecture, I begin to think that the audience will be very appreciative of my presentation, and they will like very much some of the ideas I will be bringing to them, I will be happy and excited to be giving the lecture.

Cognitive Reconstruction is aimed at taking Negative Thinking and converting it to Positive Thinking. It was like the young woman who was leaving my office to go on a job interview and said to me, "I know they won't hire me." I turned to her and said, "I know they will like you. And I know that they will hire you," at which point I stuck my tongue out at her, meaning, "Ha, ha, I'm right and you're wrong." She smiled at me and said, "You're right. I have no way of knowing that they won't like me." Our thinking is a good place to look at when we have low self-esteem, problems in everyday living, and especially when we feel depressed and anxious. Take a close look at your thinking because your thinking may be off and getting you in trouble.

Take the woman who was constantly getting abused by other people. First, she never wanted to tell people that they were hurting her feelings ("Why give them the satisfaction of knowing that they hurt me"), and secondly, she felt she was demeaning herself by admitting that her feelings were hurt. Hence, people either did not know they were hurting her, or they were allowed to escape from being confronted, and in reality she continued to be hurt. By changing her thinking, from a negative projected outcome to a positive anticipated outcome, she began to think more effectively and more positively. She began telling people how she felt. Before long people got the message and tried not to hurt her feelings. It was a change in her thinking that allowed her to communicate what she was feeling that caused other people to take notice and refrain from hurting her feelings. Examine your own thinking and see if you can spot your own negative thinking. By doing cognitive reconstruction, converting negative thinking to positive thinking, you will take a giant step toward helping yourself along that difficult road to health and wellness.

Postscript

If we stand back and take a look at what is happening in our daily lives, over a period of time we begin to see trends that we did not see before. A good example of this phenomenon occurred to all of us when we were growing up. Can you remember people coming up to you and telling you how much you have grown since the last time they saw you? That's exactly what I am referring to. Small changes take place on a daily basis but may not be observable unless we look for them.

So the next time you wake up and go out and face the world, be observant, take a good look at what is happening around you. Check out to see who is behaving in which way, who is aware of his or her own feelings and thinking, and who is tuned out. Furthermore, become aware of how tuned in you yourself are. Remember, being aware is the first step in helping us become successful in life.

Unfortunately, what you most probably will observe will be absolutely amazing, how many of us are walking around in our daily lives totally oblivious as to who we are, what we are feeling or thinking, and certainly unaware what the other guy is thinking or feeling. By the way, there will be that contingent who will tell you, "Who cares about what other people are thinking or feeling... I don't want to know what I am thinking or feeling, so why should I want to know what others are feeling or thinking?" As Chapter 6 teaches us, unless we are aware of what is inside of us, we run the risk of becoming mentally and physically susceptible to illness. Therefore, the question becomes: Where can we go to learn this emotional intelligence which will help us stay physically and mentally healthy as well as give us a boost in becoming successful in life? In as much as managed care has managed to eliminate long term psychotherapy, we cannot learn enough of it in short term psychotherapy to carry us through to manifest itself in successful everyday living. Today we can only learn pieces of it in psychotherapy. So where do we go to learn it?

The two remaining places where most of us learned, aside from what we learned from "the street" (and no one on the street has the knowledge to teach it to us anyway), is in our families and in our schools. Families must become aware of how important it is to teach its members Awareness, Communication, and Conflict Resolution. Inasmuch as there are so many pressures on young families, often with both parents working, our public and private schools need to take the initiative to convert from a cognitive teaching approach to a more emotionally based teaching approach. Hence, the burden falls heavily on both our families and our schools to begin to focus more on thinking and feeling than on behavior alone and cognitive learning alone.

While some of these transactions are taking place, some of us have been advocating them for decades. Described as "a prominent psychologist," I was quoted in a national magazine article in 1972 as saying children should be taught how to live happy and mentally healthy lives. "Each year we somehow manage to graduate students more emotionally disturbed than in previous years," I said then (and I still say now). "We spend a great deal of time and effort in educating the talent but very little in educating the emotions...Preventive psychology courses should be taught from kindergarten to 12th grade. They should be part of the curriculum. And it should be done now. As things in society get more complex, the tensions of everyday living increase...Marriages fail, suicides increase; there is more alienation, dehumanization, more isolation of the individual. Students graduate, go off to college, and have mental breakdowns...We spend a lot of money building community health centers to cure people society has made sick but we'd be better off spending more on teaching people to avoid psychological problems."

Today, so many years after I was quoted above, the message remains the same. By focusing on the emotional aspects of life by concentrating on Awareness, Communication, and Conflict Resolution, our chances of achieving a happy, successful life improve dramatically.

Success in life starts with acquiring knowledge and then applying that knowledge to everyday living. Our own awareness plays a large part in helping us focus our attention on where we go to acquire that knowledge. The pages that precede this postscript are intended to provide the reader with psychological knowledge that will give us The Psychological Edge, the psychological advantage. What you, the reader, do with this knowledge is extremely important. Just as in psychotherapy, no one gets cured in the consultation room; success takes place in putting into practice what the patient has learned in the office. Putting this psychological knowledge to work for you is hard work. It means working and re-working old, long-established patterns, habits that are hard to break. Nonetheless, the rewards are enormous, both psychologically and physically. In fact, our whole sense of well being very much depends upon what we do with the knowledge that we acquire.

Good luck. Go to it. Do it. When you get bogged down, go back to the pages that will help you work through the resistance. Develop The Psychological Edge. It could add years to your life.